Which? Way to Drive Your Small Business

About the author

Lynn Brittney, who has worked in public relations, publishing and as a lecturer, has written articles for various magazines and journals as well as several books. Her other books include a series of Directors' Guides for the Institute of Directors, *Intelligent Manufacturing* (Addison Wesley) and *Successful Conferences and Other Business Events* (WEKA Publishing), and, for Foulsham, *Study Time Management* and *A Woman Alone*. She is the author of *The Which? Guide to Domestic Help* and *The Which? Guide to Working from Home*.

Which? Way to Drive Your Small Business

Lynn Brittney

 CONSUMERS' ASSOCIATION

Which? Books are commissioned and researched by
Consumers' Association and published by
Which? Ltd, 2 Marylebone Road, London NW1 4DF
Email address: books@which.net

Distributed by The Penguin Group:
Penguin Books Ltd, 27 Wrights Lane, London W8 5TZ

The author and publishers would like to thank the following for their help in the preparation
of this book: Andy Brenan and Chris Rawlins (British Bankers' Association), British Venture
Capital Association, Ian Foyster, Rebecca Fearnley, Andy Hardy, Jonquil Lowe, Roger Moore,
TM Services Emergency Response Training

First edition May 2001

British Library Cataloguing in Publication Data
A catalogue record for this book is available from the British Library

ISBN 0 85202 855 5

For a full list of *Which?* books, please write to Which? Books, Castlemead, Gascoyne Way,
Hertford X, SG14 1LH or access our web site at *www.which.net*

Cover and text design by Kysen Creative Consultants
Cover photograph by Steve Taylor/Tony Stone Images

Typeset by Saxon Graphics Ltd, Derby
Printed and bound in Great Britain by Clays Ltd, Bungay, Suffolk

Contents

★An asterisk next to the name of an organisation in the text indicates that the address can be found in this section

Introduction

This book examines the choices facing small and medium enterprises (SMEs) – the government's definition for businesses with up to 249 employees. Thousands of small businesses start up in Britain each year. A significant proportion of them fail by the end of their first year of operation, and the majority of businesses close before their third birthday. In 2000, according to Dun and Bradstreet, the business information service, 40,847 businesses ceased trading. Many of them were in the manufacturing sector, and manufacturers which collapse often take with them a clutch of small businesses that were their customers. However, despite these depressing statistics a large number of new businesses *do* survive and carry on to be successful, thriving concerns, many of which expand and diversify from their core business.

How do these businesses survive beyond those first, critical years, and what is the key to their success? This book will answer these questions by looking at the common pitfalls that all businesses face and drawing upon the experience of those who overcame the stumbling blocks and went on to greater prosperity.

There is no doubt that careful planning in the start-up phase can stand businesses in good stead. Contingency planning is often overlooked in the rush of enthusiasm and the initial success of a business idea. But it is something companies overlook at their peril. Sometimes small businesses might plan for the easily insurable disasters such as theft, illness of key employees, fire, flood and other natural disasters, but they may not lay down plans for coping with sudden and overwhelming success. The demands of a huge, unexpected manufacturing order can totally wipe out an emerging cottage industry. Alternatively, the restriction of cashflow caused by one major client not paying on time can be devastating in the first few years of operation.

Other errors could include a reluctance to take professional help and advice at key points along the road of development; or, at the other end of the scale, responding too eagerly to pressure from 'experts' who tell a company that it will fail without the latest technology. As this guide demonstrates, a business needs to be healthy first and make appropriate choices in order to benefit from the latest developments.

Another problem can be reluctance on the part of the business's owner to delegate tasks to employees and allow him- or herself time to run the company. An inability to take on board the ideas and suggestions of employees – who can make a significant contribution to company growth – may also need to be overcome.

In today's climate, one of the strongest brakes on the development of small companies is the stranglehold of bureaucracy. In 1999 the government created a staggering 3,468 new regulations for businesses, causing the Shadow Leader of the Commons, Angela Browning, to comment: 'The cost of regulation and red tape falls heaviest on small businesses that do not have in-house accountants, lawyers and personnel directors. The person trying to run the business has to deal with all this bureaucracy and that is where it starts to affect their ability to grow the business and be competitive.' Chapter 12 explains how to keep up to date with legislation and minimise the inconvenience of administering rules and regulations.

Running a company depends on cultivating a positive outlook. Essentially, the hurdle between success and failure is vaulted by a combination of professional attitude and ambition. The most dynamic entrepreneurs think ahead on a grand scale. This requires a change in perception – a willingness to adapt to changes which will take you from one-person start-up to managing director of a large company. You need to decide how large you want your company to grow (this may change with time). If you want life to stay the same you should choose to stay small and contain your operation. However, any small business that decides to do this must recognise that it may mean limiting the life of the company.

Of course, all businesses have different requirements. *Which? Way to Drive Your Small Business* outlines the choices that have to be made at this crucial stage of development and, once you have decided how to take your business forward, it provides you with the tools to allow you to rise to the challenges along the way.

Chapter 1

Planning for growth

The percentage of casualties amongst small- to medium-sized businesses (SMEs) during the first two years of operation is high. Almost 50 per cent do not make it to the third year, for a variety of reasons. Many of these casualties fail as a result of inexperience, bad planning, cash shortages, poor marketing and/or lack of resources. The reality is that too many people rush into business with what seems like a good idea but turns out to be unworkable in practice, or with a basically sound idea for which they lack the experience, or resources, to manage successfully.

This is a book for those who have survived beyond the difficult start-up period and want to develop their business further. Reaching the stage where the business is ready to expand is another accident black spot. Expansion requires as much thought, planning and resource as the initial setting-up, and can be more difficult. Many SMEs find themselves stuck between the proverbial rock and a hard place. On the one hand, it is dangerous to do nothing and run the risk of the business dying on its feet through lack of development. On the other, it is foolhardy to expand without having the right support systems in place.

Where is your business now?

This guide assumes that you have arrived at a point where you are reasonably confident that your business is going to survive. The Institute of Management (IM)* has defined this stage in terms of the company being probably 'more than two years old, since you have to be sure that what worked the first year can be repeated in the second year. Once you have been through two tax years and can show at least a small profit then you know you have a foundation business which can be built upon.' Statistics from March 2000 showed that the majority of new businesses close before they are

9

three years old, so reaching this point can be considered something of a landmark.

Your initial business plan, the one that you drew up when you started your business, should have shown where you expected to be after being up and running for two years. That business plan, of course, was drawn up not just to convince others that you had a worthwhile business idea, or to impress your bank manager, but as your blueprint – a map showing how your business could chart its course through the often choppy seas of the business world.

So, have you looked at your business plan lately? Does the initial ambition match up to the reality, two or more years on? Now is the time to take stock, redraw that business plan and set yourself some new goals.

Your new business plan

The great thing about drawing up a new business plan after a couple of years in operation is that none of it should be estimated any more, because you now hold hard facts and figures as well as real market knowledge and experience of how your business operates. It can be interesting to go through that first business plan and compare, say, your planned marketing strategy at start-up with the real strategy that you have had to develop as your company has developed. Look, for example, at how many developments were planned and how much was the result of contigency.

The business plan should contain:

- **an executive summary** This should state the current position of the business, its customers and projected sales, and why you think you will achieve these projected sales. (As this is just the summary, a couple of lines will do here.) You should state the short-, medium- and long-term objectives of the business and how you plan to achieve them. Include a summary of financial forecasts and how much money you may need to achieve your goals. If you discover that you do not actually have any objectives, other than to keep going, then you are, without a doubt, in trouble. In order for a business to be successful it has to develop, evolve, seek new markets, set new goals, perhaps expand – but *never* stay the same. Virtually every business that stays the same stagnates and eventually dies

- **an explanation of the nature of the business** The next part of the business plan should be a detailed explanation of what your business is and does. Has this changed since you started up? For example, you might have started out as an energy consultancy but along the way found gaps in the market and seized those opportunities, employing other types of consultants to broaden the scope of your company's services. It is worth contrasting the description of your company now with the original description – this is a good way of charting the evolution of your business

- **a description of your product or service** This should include more detail about what exactly you are selling and how you hope to develop your core product or your range. If your company has evolved since start-up then the specifications are very likely to have changed. Have you added more to your product line? Have you enlarged or perhaps redefined your services? This is where you should record your hopes for the future inasmuch as it will impact on your product or service

- **an outline of operations** The nitty-gritty of how your company works – i.e. the structure, the processes, the production methods, the client contact, the presentation of the end result. Your entry here should make a fascinating contrast to the start-up business plan, now that you are dealing in real as opposed to 'hoped-for' operations. Here also is a place to indicate future plans. How do you see those operational processes changing? Perhaps you will need to invest in technology to offer the marketplace what it wants

- **an overview of your market and your competitors** This section should be much more detailed than it was in the original plan. You will now have established your markets, perhaps creating new ones or abandoning original ones in the process. Some of your competitors may have proved too strong for you and you might have been forced to move out of their marketplace into another. You may have held your own, or even beaten some of the opposition – with either skilful marketing or pricing, or by developing a better product or service. If your business has survived more than two years then you are probably streetwise enough to have your eye on yet more market opportunities. You need to identify these, justifying why it is appropriate that your business tackles them

- **a marketing plan** Your start-up marketing plan will probably look fairly simplistic compared to your current strategy – perhaps laughably so. Now that you have a background of experience and know what works and what does not, you can go into detail. In your research to find new markets, plan for expansion and grow the business, you are also likely to have looked at new ways of marketing. You may have watched your competitors come unstuck by investing heavily in the Internet as a means of marketing only to find that it did not work as well as traditional methods. You may have dabbled in advertising on television and got your fingers burnt. You will probably have made mistakes, maybe expensive ones, but you will have learnt from them by the time you re-do your business plan, and should be all the better prepared to drive your business ahead

- **financial forecasts** You will see a big difference here. Your accountants will find the production of sales forecasts and cash-flow forecasts relatively easy compared to the 'pull-figures-out-of-the-air' technique of start-up business plans. Now you can assemble real, not estimated, figures and you can base future projections on base-line figures from your current financial situation

- **financial analysis** The profit and loss and balance sheet forecasts will, similarly, be constructed on solid data. These will enable you, and any potential investor or lender, to accurately gauge how much financial commitment your ambitions will cost you.

Once you have drawn up this 'statement of intent' you can then spend some time thinking about how you are going to achieve the proposed development.

Developing your company

The business plan is your blueprint, but there are many other facets to developing a successful company. A business plan tells you and others what you *want* to do. It doesn't necessarily tell you *how* to achieve it, other than predicating the need to get your sums right.

Your major asset

The major factor in the running of any business is the quality of its staff – the co-operation, skills, loyalty, creativity, commitment, reliability and diligence of employees can take a company from nothing to a world-class company in no time at all – a fact that is underestimated by too many businesses. This book devotes considerable space to the importance of developing the quality of both management and staff. In fact, almost every chapter has some advice on the human resources element of business development, which is so crucial to its success.

Management skills

It is not just the quality of staff that is important, but the quality of management. Enlightened owners and managers of businesses realise that they have to develop themselves as well as their business. Chapter 3, for example, discusses learning from others – either in a structured programme, such as benchmarking, or through an individual arrangement with a mentor. Benchmarking, of course, is not just a management exercise. It should be illuminating for the whole company to learn from the successes of others. However, as we all know, nothing can be entered into without management commitment. Owner/managers can bear the brunt of driving a business. With the many demands placed upon them, it is crucial for employers to look after themselves as well as their staff (see Chapter 14).

E-commerce and technology

Many companies have made the mistake of assuming that technology holds most of the solutions to business problems. In fact, although it may solve some problems, it is counter-productive if it is bolted on to a shaky infrastructure. Using technology and e-commerce is discussed in Chapter 5.

Be inspired and effective

Companies cannot succeed without being creative and proactive. This demands good communication and the sharing of knowledge. Even the most junior member of staff should have the confidence to contribute to the development of ideas and knowledge within the company. The lines between management and employees very often have to be blurred now that businesses increasingly rely on multi-tasking teams, and few SMEs can afford to carry managers who do not have a productive function within a company. The principles of knowledge management are covered in Chapter 4, which also gives advice on creating an innovative business and improving customer relations and operational procedures.

The burden of red tape

Owner/managers of SMEs have their work cut out, now and in the future. The amount of legislation only seems to get heavier. Despite representation to the government and the EU by organisations representing businesses, the laws and regulations continue to multiply, particularly in the area of employment. The year 2001 has seen the introduction of paid paternity leave, enhanced maternity leave and pressure from the government to introduce greater support for working parents through flexible working hours. Keeping on top of all this legislation is just one of the many balls that SMEs have to keep in the air as they juggle the demands of their business. Chapter 7 discusses dealing with the tax authorities, and Chapter 12 looks at significant developments in employment law.

Ensuring a solid foundation

Before you can drive your business ahead, the foundations must be secure. Everything must be in place if it is to develop into a stronger organisation that can meet any challenges. This requires a careful analysis of your current market position, threats (such as new competition, or legislation that will significantly increase your cost base), weaknesses, strengths, financial status and future needs, amongst other things. In addition to a thorough audit of your business, you may need some expert advice. This book will point you in the right direction.

General help for small businesses

Despite the mushrooming bureaucracy SMEs must deal with, it would be wrong to think that the government is out to kill off businesses. In fact, a lot of government-sponsored help for businesses is available. Whilst only a small percentage of businesses may qualify for grants or special loans (see Chapter 9 for more information), *all* businesses can avail themselves of the many advisory organisations that dispense information free of charge, or for a relatively modest fee can sort out matters such as business plans, incubating or developing a business, finding a mentor or putting you in touch with potential investors.

This book distils much of this valuable advice so that owner/managers approaching that all-important period of growth and development will quickly find the information they need.

Government bodies

Both the Department of Trade and Industry* (DTI) and the Small Business Service* (SBS) have a wide range of information, publications and services on offer to businesses, including useful web sites.

The Small Business Service is an executive agency of the DTI offering support and advice to firms on finance, skills acquisition and improving efficiency. From April 2001 some local outlets are being established in England.

At the time of writing, TECs (Training and Enterprise Councils) and LECs (Local Enterprise Councils) specialise in administering the many initiatives that help business proprietors to train their workforces more effectively. The remit of the TECs is currently in the process of being transferred to the Learning and Skills Council (LSC)* and Small Business Service.

Business Link

The DTI works closely with these local business advice units, which offer advice to SMEs. They are known as Business Links in England (call the Business Link* signpost number or look on the web site for details of your nearest centre), and as Small Business Gateway* in lowland Scotland and Business Information Source* in the Highlands and Islands of Scotland. Business Connect* offices exist in Wales while in Northern Ireland you can contact the Local Enterprise Development Unit (LEDU)* or EDnet (the Economic Development Network).*

These local business advice centres understand the needs of SMEs in their particular regions. They are the best point of contact for information about grants, loans, business services and opportunities.

Enterprise Agencies

Enterprise Agencies (Enterprise Trusts in Scotland) are independent organisations which offer help with starting up and running an SME successfully. To find your nearest agency, contact the National Federation of Enterprise Agencies★ or your local Business Link, or look in *Yellow Pages* under 'Business Enterprise Agencies'. Enterprise Agencies can advise business people on finance, marketing and training.

Technology and innovation

If you are considering developing your business using new technology (and that does not just mean computers) then the UK Business Incubation Centre★ may be able to provide advice. The UK Science Park Association (UKSPA)★ can put you in touch with one of the 50 Science Parks around the UK.

The National Endowment for Science, Technology and the Arts (NESTA)★ aims to help creative individuals develop ideas effectively and is a source of financial support. The Institute of Patentees and Inventors★ offers advice on inventing and protecting business ideas, while the Patent Office★ can supply information about patents, copyright and trademarks.

These are just a few of the contact points that are available. Relevant sources of help are mentioned throughout this book. For more general information, contact the DTI Support for Business web site at *www.dti.gov.uk/support/index.htm*

Chapter 2

Avoiding the classic reasons for business failure

What makes a company fail a short time after it got off to what looked like such a good start? The office of the Official Receiver lists the following as the most common reasons for businesses to fail:

- not enough capital
- not selling enough
- bad management
- taking too much cash out of the business too early
- poor accounting
- lack of experience
- bad debts
- setting prices too low
- over-extending the business
- fraud
- operating costs getting out of hand
- poor supervision
- competition
- health problems of the owner.

These factors will be referred to throughout this book. Meanwhile, this chapter will look at each cause of failure, examine it more closely and see how it could have been avoided.

Not enough capital
For businesses that are going through a period of growth, diversification or reinvention, this is a common reason for failure. Frequently, the cost of such changes is underestimated by inexperienced owners who are moving away from their familiar

core activity – the knitwear manufacturer who moves into mail order, for example, and has no experience of the expense involved in setting up this completely new arm of the business. New people will have to be employed to deal with a venture that requires sales and administrative staff. New computer systems are needed to deal with direct sales to consumers who are paying by a variety of procedures – cash, credit card, cheque or invoice. In addition various types of costs accrue: first and foremost, promotional costs, but also despatch costs, the cost of returns, the cost of building up a customer base, the cost of chasing small bad debts and the cost of pricing errors. A diversification option which seems so simple can prove complex and expensive, and inadequate preparation can cause tremendous cashflow problems for the core business.

The small publisher

A very small publishing company in the West Country comprising a husband and wife and one employee made a reasonable profit selling walking guides to ramblers and hikers through specialist magazines, walking holiday operators and local hotels. The books were produced on computers using a DTP system, with hand-drawn maps scanned on to the pages. The printed pages were then photocopied, stapled into handbook form with card covers and despatched. The whole process kept overheads to a minimum, did not involve the use of printing companies and costs were contained. However, the company realised that it would have to grow and diversify in order to keep ahead of the game, so it decided to go into more comprehensive guides for travellers, which would be marketed through local tourist boards and other outlets. But this audience demanded colour illustrations as well as text, which made the books more substantial. Because the new guides required proper binding it became necessary to deal with printing companies. This required considerably more liquid cash. After seeking advice from the local Business Link, the company set up a loan facility with its bank under the Small Business Service (SBS)* Small Firms Loan Guarantee System, and had its accounting system taken over by a professional accountant. This set it up with sufficient cash to implement a growth plan and provided the infrastructure to monitor cashflow.

Businesses should always seek professional advice when assessing their needs for working and investment capital. Banks, accountants or Business Link* advice units (see page 15) can help with this assessment procedure. The best policy is to appoint someone who can evaluate the business and identify its strengths and weaknesses with regard to cashflow, profit, turnover, investment and overheads. This evaluation will form the basis of a business plan which will outline the direction in which you hope your business will develop over the next five to ten years (see Chapter 1). Managing the money is discussed in greater depth in Chapter 7. Meanwhile, bear in mind two golden rules:

1 in your enthusiasm to get a project off the ground, never underestimate how much it is going to cost
2 be totally honest to yourself and your advisers about every financial movement in your company.

Not selling enough

If you do not sell you do not earn. Frequently, problems occur when a company has developed from a one-man band and the owner used to do everything personally. Overcoming the profound belief that no one can sell the company's products or services like the person who created the business in the first place is one of the biggest hurdles owners have to face. There comes a time when you have to concentrate on running the company and let others do the selling.

Options include employing highly skilled salespeople, using a telesales shop (if your business can be done over the phone), the Internet or a marketing consultancy. It has been known for some owners to regard sales as such a personal platform that they unconsciously hire inadequate salespeople out of a perverse desire to see them fail. If you let ego get in the way of success the failure will be yours and no one else's.

An owner who is a great salesperson is best advised to use his talent to investigate the market and make strategic decisions which can be communicated to employees who will go out and do the actual selling. Conversely, a lack of sales can be the result of an owner/manager who is primarily a manufacturer or creative person trying to sell when his or her talents do not lie in that direction. The time comes when a professional salesperson is needed to free up everyone else to concentrate on core activities.

Often, a lack of sales reflects a lack of market research, lack of networking and failure to develop products that the customers really want. Market research has to be a continuous process in order that changes in taste or economic circumstance can be gauged, or market saturation of particular products or services anticipated. Networking – getting out and about in the industry by going to seminars, trade fairs, local chambers of commerce, etc. – can result in the development of productive relationships which might allow a company to diversify its product range, go into partnership on particular ventures or source better and cheaper suppliers, not to mention find new sales opportunities.

The office cleaning company

An office cleaning and maintenance company, although well-respected and popular, found it was losing contracts through office closures and relocations which were not replaced. No one in the company was going out actively selling the services, and advertisements in business papers, local papers and telephone directories were not having any impact. After taking advice from a marketing consultancy, the company was advised that office procurement managers were often too busy to listen and did not like to see salespeople during the working day anyway. It was suggested by the consultancy that the office cleaning company would benefit most from mass fax transmission advertising. The consultancy helped the company to draw up an effective black-and-white advertisement, then put it in touch with a company that specialised in such transmissions. The facsimile company had access to many databases covering all types and sizes of businesses. A test transmission was undertaken which produced a 9 per cent return in enquiries in one week. As a result, the senior manager of the cleaning company went to see the potential clients and secured three new contracts. Encouraged by this form of marketing, the company continued with fax adverts and employed a full-time salesperson to follow up all the enquiries.

Sales can also be enhanced by simply observing what competitors, with perhaps more money and resources at their disposal, perceive will be the new market trends. Getting out of the office or factory and into the real world can present all kinds of new opportunities and ideas.

A new approach to the way your company sells can also benefit sales. It may be that your traditional methods of marketing no longer produce results. Or that the adoption of new methods has backfired. Many companies seduced into believing that the Internet would solve all their marketing problems have since found that they need to bolster their Internet marketing with traditional brochures and catalogues sent through the mail. The Internet, for some, has proved useful merely as a gatherer of names and addresses of potential customers.

For more information about e-commerce and selling on the Internet, see Chapter 5. Chapter 6 looks at ways of expanding markets.

Bad management

The UK has a poor record of management because, historically, the education system does not prepare young people for a career in management by offering business studies as a topic early in the education process. German children, for example, can start business studies at the age of 15, while only a small percentage of UK schools offer the subject even as an A-level course.

A large proportion of UK managers just 'arrive' at the job by a process of either promotion from the ranks or via an unrelated university degree and a management training course. Industries in the UK have a low commitment to in-service training which enables employees to learn management skills as they progress in a company.

The percentage of British students who study business and management to degree level is pitiful compared with the USA, Japan or Germany. The number of successful entrepreneurs bred in the UK is also low, while the number of business failures due to bad management is high.

What is a bad manager? Look at the checklist overleaf and be honest with yourself.

A bad manager:

- makes uninformed decisions
- fails to listen to employees' suggestions and ideas
- does not understand the accounts when they are presented
- does not know what the company's cashflow situation is at any given time
- has a distant relationship with employees, preferring management by memo to face-to-face contact
- does not embrace change
- is not prepared to spend money on staff training
- does not put effort into developing customer relationships
- indulges in nepotism and grants special favours to friends
- spends a lot of time out of the company during the working week on personal business
- spies on employees and criticises their work without offering constructive feedback
- authorises extravagant expenditure on corporate hospitality but begrudges spending money on new equipment or training
- does not supervise under-managers properly
- neglects to arrange regular meetings at which the company's operations or future developments can be discussed with staff
- does not motivate employees or reward hard work
- fails to seek the advice of professionals or admit ignorance in certain business areas
- takes too much cash out of the business for his own salary and perks but pays staff poorly.

Do not let your company become a failure due to poor management training and development. From looking at the list above you can probably draw your own conclusions about what makes a good manager. It is necessary in today's climate to make a conscious effort to refine your management skills – a fact that many owner/managers of SMEs tend to overlook in the pressure of day-to-day business.

Relationships with staff are important. How they perceive your contribution to the company, other than being the person who set it all up, is an important part of how they perform under your management. It is not always necessary, or desirable, for the managing director or other directors to be 'best buddies' with the rest of the staff in order to achieve a good working relationship. Respect – an old-fashioned word but none the less valid – is the keystone of how well people work for their managers. Respect can be more easily formed for managers who are known to have more knowledge than their staff; equal or better skills; an ability to appreciate the complexity of work demanded of others; and, most importantly, show consideration for their staff. Respect begets respect.

There are some things that can be learnt and others that cannot. Personal skills such as empathy are probably innate, although some human resource specialists might argue that they can be taught. Managers can, of course, take advantage of the many courses and seminars in management techniques offered by organisations like the Institute of Directors (IoD)* or the Institute of Management (IM).* However, beware of becoming a professional attender of courses. There is little point in learning skills if you are never around to put them into practice.

Taking too much cash out of the business too early

Frequently this is directly linked to bad management. The greed or need of the business owner and his or her family can cripple an emerging business. Many of the early dotcom failures could be put down to the fact that the owners demanded a very high standard of living even though their companies were in their infancies. Two or three partners requiring start-off salaries of £100,000 a year or more does not give a new business a chance. Situating your fledgling company in a designer loft in central London is too much of a burden on overheads. Bill Gates and many of the other computer software billionaires started off living at home with their parents or operating out of a garage. The big houses, fancy cars and architect-designed offices came later. A good adviser, plus a large dollop of common sense, should tell anyone developing a business that, in the early years, it is best to keep your needs modest and plough any profits back into the company, investing in whatever you know will make it prosper – for example, new equipment, staff training or product development.

Obviously, staff who see a fledgling company being sucked dry by its owners will feel neither commitment nor loyalty to it. They will be painfully aware that all the owners are interested in is short-term personal gain rather than building a company with a future.

Sometimes, a cash drain is not due to greed but a genuine mistake on the part of the owner/manager who falls prey to over-enthusiasm, bad advice or an uninformed decision. A small company which sees an opportunity to grow or diversify requires capital. Owners who take cash from the emerging core business rather than seeking advice and perhaps borrowing the necessary amounts may end up crippling everything after they run out of money.

The computer software company

A small five-person company was run by young, inexperienced but enthusiastic software designers. They created two successful pieces of software which, for the first two years of operation, kept their business in reasonable profit. But the three owners of the company became restless and were persuaded to invest large amounts of money in buying in other software designs over the next two years, rather than creating them in-house. Most of these external software designs were faulty and had to be expensively re-programmed or, in some cases, abandoned. Although a disproportionate amount of money had been spent in purchasing these products, only one made it to the market, where it failed through lack of marketing. The company itself collapsed after five years. It had taken too much cash out of the initially successful business too early, instead of following business plans that allowed for affordable investment and growth in the right economic climate.

If proper advice is followed, expenditure on growth can benefit a business. Chapter 9 describes ways of raising capital and the types of grant available, while Chapter 10 looks at ways of expanding your company.

Poor accounting

This is another area where sentiment can overrule common sense. Many a small business has started off with the owner's spouse doing the books, more or less competently. But there comes a point in a business's development where bookkeeping has to give way to proper accounting. A good accountant should be able to read the company's figures like a map of the world. These figures will show:

- where the business is top-heavy (too many chiefs on big salaries and not enough workers)
- where the overheads are beginning to bite (e.g. office rents getting out of hand)
- where purchasing costs could be lowered (e.g. you could buy supplies more cheaply over the Internet or negotiate a special rate on something you use a lot of)
- where to anticipate the lowest point of cashflow in the year (if your sales are seasonal, you may need an overdraft to pay the bills off-season)
- where the pricing of products is wrong (you may need to restructure the costs of items being sold overseas if despatch costs are cutting into the profit margin)
- where money can be found for new ventures, salary increases, more supplies etc.

A good accountant can suggest ways of saving money – for example, through changing the company's tax year to take advantage of seasonal highs and lows, and through buying banking services at the best possible rate. But, most important, a good accountant can act as devil's advocate, serving to temper enthusiasm for, say, the latest scheme or piece of technology with sound advice about the *real* costs of the undertaking. Also, an accountant can draw up 'what if?' scenarios to show how a business can grow or cope with emergencies by changing its buying habits or wage levels, or through investment back into the company in various ways.

To find a good accountant, whether fulltime or in an auditor/consultant role, follow the recommendations of business associates or friends. The best accountants will have many satisfied clients who can sing their praises (make sure that these clients are reputable companies with good track records). Check that any accountant you are thinking of using is a member of an appropriate professional body, such as the Association of Chartered Certified Accountants,* and is known to your bank and local business organisations.

Lack of experience
Three types of inexperience in an owner can render a business vulnerable:

- inability to keep a good idea afloat or diversify
- failure to comprehend all the issues involved in running a company
- lack of sound business knowledge – or even plain common sense.

The first sort of lack of experience is failure to capitalise on a winning formula. For example, someone may be very creative and get a really good idea or spot an excellent gap in the market. For the first year of the business, everything might seem to go well. But, eventually, the good idea may founder – because, say, it had a limited lifespan and the company should have diversified or enlarged its product base before interest petered out.

The second form of lack of experience is failing to understand what is involved in running a small business. People who make this mistake tend to believe that they are, in fact, *very* experienced because they have set up their own business in an industry where they have worked for many years, which they feel they know inside out. They have the contacts, they know where to sell their products or services, they know the idiosyncrasies of that marketplace. They seem to have all the experience in the world but what they do not have, of course, is experience of running their own business. Before, they have always been an employee. They may not have had to make difficult decisions, employ people, understand the accounts, deal with banks or cope with the pressure of keeping a business going in a time of crisis. It is a whole new ball game and while some people take to it like a duck to water, many more founder under the overwhelming responsibility of it all. For example, the creative person who had a good idea may run a business inefficiently with the result that the company runs out of money, ideas and customers. The answer is for that person to recognise his or her limitations and find a non-executive director, a mentor (see page 43) or a partner who can help with the day-to-day running of the business.

The third kind is probably the worst – total lack of experience. This includes people who buy a business, like a small hotel or a pub, because they think that anyone can run one and they have 'always fancied it'. But they have never run a business before, of any kind, and they have no concept of how difficult such a venture will be.

The English Tourist Board reports that there are a huge number of failures in the tourist industry each year, simply because new entrants to the business come to it armed with little more than, say, a rosy idea of running a small hotel. When they find out what back-breaking, demanding work it is, they throw in the towel. It is a similar story with franchises. Many people fail to take advice before purchasing a franchise and end up regretting it. (To find out whether franchising is for you, see page 152.)

The best solution to this problem is caution on the part of those keen to try a new venture. Of course, there is nothing to stop anyone rushing out and buying a free house or a small hotel but it would be foolish to do so without some training beforehand. Many organisations – such as the brewery/hospitality companies that own pubs and hotels and the English Tourist Board – as well as franchisers now insist on would-be entrepreneurs attending training courses and seminars and doing on-the-job apprenticeships before they are even considered as candidates to take on certain businesses.

For more information contact the Brewers and Licensed Retailers Association (BLRA)★ or your regional Tourist Board. You could also check whether your local adult education institute runs hotel management and catering courses, or other vocational classes.

Bad debts

This is the saddest reason for business failure because bad debts are often no fault of the small business itself. The latest statistics (at the end of 2000) regarding business failures report that closures are highest amongst manufacturers, particularly in the north of England. Every medium-to-large manufacturer that shuts down may take a handful or more of small businesses with it because the company has not been able to pay them. The likelihood of this happening increases if those small businesses are caught in the trap of having just one or two large clients instead of several small ones. If you are heavily reliant on supplying a few large clients, you could go under when they do because most of your income will be wiped out at once. As mentioned earlier in this chapter, networking is the best way to increase your client base. Get out there and talk to people. Go to trade fairs and exhibitions, join business groups – put your company's name about.

Sometimes, businesses find that an accumulation of small bad debts eats away into any potential profit margin. The number of businesses, for example, offering television rental has dwindled – firstly because most people own their own televisions now and secondly because the companies spent so much time and money chasing payment defaulters that it became obvious that there was no money to be made in this sector.

Setting prices too low

Pricing products successfully is a hard thing to do. Even big, well-established companies such as Marks & Spencer come unstuck (see opposite).

Several factors affect the pricing of a product. First and foremost, it must cover the costs of manufacture, processing, administration, marketing, storage, despatch, overheads etc. and should leave you with a modest profit at the end of it. Secondly, the price must be right for the intended market. Pitch it too high and it will lose out to cheaper competitors; pitch it too low and it will be viewed with suspicion and probably suspected to be of inferior quality. Thirdly, the price of a product, in whatever market segment, has to be competitive. It has to reflect the price of similar products around it – it is for you to decide whether the price should be the same (in which case it is advisable that the product has added features in order to win out), or whether the price should undercut the competition (in which case the product may need an aggressive sales technique).

Many companies approach pricing from the wrong end. They say 'We want to sell this product or service and we cannot charge more for it than X' – then they try to make the company squeeze a profit out of the product even though it may be time-consuming or expensive to make and will never be able to generate enough revenue to be cost-effective. A good accountant (see page 25) or consultant could help here, by examining various products or services to see which of them would generate the best return for the company. This would be the first step in developing a sound costing and pricing policy. The ultimate decision might be, for example, that low-cost, high-turnover, mass-market goods are not viable, even though they cost less to make, because the profit made from each item is so minimal that the company would be better off concentrating on quality items that can be aimed at a less price-sensitive market. It is a particular failing in craft industries that small businesses neglect to reflect realistically in the price of craft items the amount of time they have taken to create.

In theory, you cannot set a price that is too high, if you aim it at the right market. No one demurs about paying over £1,000 for a pair of Manolo Blahnik shoes because the shoes are high-quality, exclusive designs and only marketed to people to whom money is no object. The problem comes when your company's image and market appeal is at odds with your pricing structure.

The milliner

A small business in the south-east of England is owned by a woman who designs hats and employs six female homeworkers who sew and trim her designs. The business is highly profitable because the owner knew from the start that the hats that she wanted to produce were labour-intensive and expensive. Having worked out the economics of running a business based on hats for the high-street mass market, she knew she would not be able to get the pricing structure right for those customers. Therefore she decided to make limited editions of each hat design and also make individual designer hats on request. The exclusiveness of her designs was reflected in the high price of the hats, which were marketed successfully through magazines such as *Country Life* and *Tatler* to women who attend many high-profile social functions a year.

Marks & Spencer ran into difficulties over its pricing policy. The company has a long history of high-street, mass-market presence and a reputation for quality. However, part of its problem in the late 1990s was that consumers did not want to pay the prices M&S were charging for clothes that were generally thought to be dull. When M&S decided to produce, for example, beige cashmere sweaters costing over £150, it lost touch with its core market. Its customers did not want cashmere, nor could they afford the prices. If they wanted a plain beige sweater they could go to other high-street stores and buy one for £10. Those that could afford and wanted cashmere would not have dreamt of buying it in a high-street chain like M&S. The company subsequently introduced an upmarket 'designer' strand to its business which failed to improve sales, was forced to close all its French branches and is currently undergoing major reorganisation.

Over-extending the business

There is a great temptation, if you are riding a wave of success following the initial business set-up, to add to your 'empire' when any interesting or feasible suggestion or opportunity presents itself. However, any change, redefinition, diversification or expansion requires a cash injection to put the necessary infrastructure in place. Some banks, judging by the number that willingly extended loans, overdrafts and yet more overdrafts to the many dotcom companies that subsequently failed within a very short space of time, are only too willing to prop up a dream with cash if it is exciting enough – and just as eager to call in the debt when they feel a business is over-extended. For advice on obtaining finance, see Chapter 8.

Many investors became overwhelmingly enthusiastic about the Internet, ploughing money into all kinds of ventures which, in reality, were based on nothing more than ideas put up by young, inexperienced (but IT-competent) people. When the dotcom boom occurred, e-tailing (selling on the Net) had no track record, there were precious few hard market statistics and everyone believed that the vast American market of 'surfers' would buy anything if it was sold on the Web. No one said, as they would have done with a low-tech business, 'Do not fill warehouses with goods – you may never sell them. Proceed cautiously. Wait until you have established a regular market before you increase your orders to suppliers.' No. They said, 'The sky's the limit. Go for it. 100 million people could log on to your web site and buy from you'. But this did not happen and many companies ran out of cash, or are still trading, as we go to press, but are still not making profits. Chapter 5 looks at the potential risks and rewards of e-commerce.

Many publishing and toy manufacturers have been caught out by being tempted to go into the unfamiliar area of film and television merchandising. Fashions and passions change quickly, particularly in the children's marketplace. No sooner has one blockbuster film come out than another is hot on its tail. The sight of *Star Wars – The Phantom Menace* toys and books appearing in discount shops all over the UK is a testament to the fickleness of the children's market-place. For tips on how to be successful in the marketplace see Chapter 6.

The manufacturer of hand-painted jewellery

A reasonably prosperous cottage industry, set up by one individual with his redundancy money, produced cufflinks and pendants made from hand-enamelled old coins of the realm – threepenny bits and sixpences, etc. The owner employed approximately 15 home workers to whom he delivered the jewellery and then collected the painted items a week later. Disaster struck when he was offered the opportunity to provide the 'special offer' in a national newspaper. The newspaper ran a different offer each week and the orders were passed on to the company in question to process. The newspaper terms specified delivery within 28 days. When the offer went ahead it generated a staggering 27,000 orders in one day. The company simply could not cope. It had only 2,000 reserve stock items and the workers could only generate between them another 1,000 per week. The company ended up having to refund most of the money to customers and its reputation never recovered from the episode. Although the company kept going, it was eventually merged with a souvenir manufacturing company and the owner was bought out for very little money.

If you have one small company that is profitable then you are very much better off than the (almost) 41,000 companies that lost money and ceased trading in the year 2000. To jeopardise a healthy situation by overburdening it with quick growth is foolish. Proceed at a stately pace and you will have your empire eventually.

Fraud

Fraud is a painful experience for the victims and tragic if it results in a business closing down and people losing their livelihoods. The old chestnut that you should never trust anyone in business – not even a member of your own family – is true. Many small businesses have gone to the wall because the owners were naive, placing their trust in either a professional adviser or a customer who eventually defrauded them of large sums of money or goods. It is important to entrust the finances of your company and your personal investments only to someone who comes highly recommended, with proper references from a financial institution. Potential customers, their businesses and their credit ratings can all be checked by specialist companies before any contracts are signed or money changes hands. Any high-street bank, Enterprise Agency or Business Link★ advice unit (see page 15) can provide you with names of companies that run credit checks. Many are listed in the *Yellow Pages* and business directories. Online banks (see page 108) are now offering a service to their business customers whereby they can run credit checks online through the bank's database. Legal advisers can tell you the right questions to ask potential customers or business partners. They can also tell you how to proceed with business negotiations and contracts so that you are covered, as far as possible, against fraud.

As for family members – of course you should be able to trust them, but stories abound of chief executives who have found that their sons/daughters/wives or mistresses are guilty of embezzlement, having set up rival companies and stolen all their major customers, taken *ex gratia* payments from customers in return for lucrative contracts, and so on.

Operating costs getting out of hand

This category involves rents and rates, salaries and perks. You also have to think about all the other costs like equipment, stationery, cars for the sales force, the running costs of vehicles for deliveries and sales, computers, telecommunications, and so on. Lean and mean is the order of the day. Pay staff well but make your corporate culture a penny-pinching one. Look to your costs. Take advice. Would investing in technology be cost-effective (see page 88)? Is leasing vehicles cheaper than buying and maintaining your own fleet? If you are in a city centre, managers are unlikely to need company cars (although company cars can be a recruitment incentive where salaries are low). Get someone to do an energy/procurement/manpower/banking audit. Find out where you can cut running costs. Many consultancies have been able to save clients hundreds of thousands of pounds a year just by helping them buy cheaper. It is a simple exercise which can yield astonishing results. Some consultancies that specialise in auditing bank statements have found that many of their clients have been consistently over-charged by banks without being aware of it – see Chapter 7. For advice on running your business more effectively see Chapter 4.

The dotcom company

Boo.com was a world-wide online retailer of fashion and sportswear, worth, on paper, £240m at its peak. The web site offered 3D images of the clothes, an electronic 'sales assistant' fluent in four languages and a virtual dressing room. The partners who founded Boo.com paid themselves huge salaries and lived lavish lifestyles. The company, which went into liquidation in spring 2000, employed nearly 500 people in high-rent offices in London, New York, Munich and Stockholm. By contrast Fashionmail, the US company that bought the operation, intends to run it with about ten people.

Poor supervision

Quality control is an important concept that does not just belong on the shop floor but in every aspect of a business, no matter what size it is.

To avoid your business developing indifferent working practices, there should be an established company policy of standards, inspections, double checking and management accountability which everyone understands. This requires:

- attention to detail by top management
- managers understanding what the jobs of employees at all levels involve, and being aware of what they are actually doing
- successful communication, so advice can be sought and given without too much delay during the working day.

Implementing such a system may initially seem time-consuming but after a while should become an acceptable part of working practices. For more on quality control see page 62.

In simple terms, a business has to be well organised and net-worked. The company policy should ensure that all workers know what is expected of them, know the rules and know that they are doing their job well. To acknowledge employees' hard work and encourage them to stay in their jobs, some employers offer incentives and operate reward schemes (see page 53).

Competition

Competition is fierce and is getting fiercer. Increased globalisation has brought the 24-hour society to us with all its attendant pressures and stresses. Markets, technologies and working practices seem to change at the speed of light. Ever since the advertising regulations were altered in the 1980s so that companies were allowed to criticise competitors' products in their advertising, the gloves have been off. Everyone is looking for an edge that will make their product or service better than the rest. Sometimes that is the problem. Businesses trying to get ahead are looking at products or services and not at the actual companies.

Today's companies need to be value-added to get an edge. They need to offer more than just the basic product or service. It is the extra-value items that are on offer – such as leisure discounts, high-street store cards, free accident insurance from banks for those who take out an account with them – which attract customers now. But in order to make customer loyalty last beyond the special offer that you are giving them at the moment, the administration, working practices and ethos of your company have to be seen to be special. Customers will develop loyalty only if the company treats them well.

You may manufacture electrical goods. Hundreds of other companies do the same. But do they offer after-sales service? Do they offer a guarantee period? Do they offer a 24-hour advice line? Your product is only as good as the customer's perception of your company. Companies that trade on the Internet are now looking at adding value by making their sites more interactive. Many companies have employed 'call centres' to manage their sites, so that customers can actually ask questions from an online salesperson and the whole sales process can be tailored to the individual's requirements. For more on customer relationships see page 54. Chapter 5 discusses selling goods via the Internet.

Fighting off the competition often depends on how well the company is managed and the type of internal culture that prevails. If products are not working for you or if services are being rejected, it may be that your employees and managers are not communicating with each other. Perhaps you are not having regular meetings to discuss progress and devoting time and energy to the research and development of your product, or encouraging creativity (see page

65). Often, you can learn how to improve your company's culture, methods and management by observing the success of others (this topic is covered in the next chapter).

Health problems of the owner

Being struck down, out of the blue, by a serious illness or accident, is something you cannot always avoid. You can make contingency plans, certainly, but it can be a hard blow for everyone concerned. In a small company the owner/manager is usually a 'hands-on' person who contributes greatly to the output of the company as a whole. It is virtually impossible to replace, at short notice, the major decision-maker, prime motivator and most valuable member of a small, close-knit team. Perhaps the chairman or MD of a large corporation might not be missed if he or she were out of action for six months following a heart attack, but in a very small company no one can be spared.

Many health problems can be avoided by not pushing yourself too hard – a common failing among owners of small to medium-sized businesses. Not delegating enough, working long hours, eating erratically, too much business travel, too many late nights, too much stress, not enough relaxation – all these can contribute to many serious illnesses. Business people are more aware nowadays of health issues but still many think that it will never happen to them, that they are the sort of people who 'thrive on stress' and 'get a buzz from the adrenaline'. Some people, like Lady Thatcher, can run a country and exist quite happily on four hours' sleep a night, but they really are rare.

People who own and run businesses have a moral obligation to look after themselves and thus ensure that the people who work for them have job security. This is discussed in greater depth in Chapter 14.

Unpredictable hazards

There are times when, no matter how wise or careful you are, things just go wrong in business. You lose a major contract because you tendered too high, or key staff defect from your company, lured by larger salaries, and take some of your best customers with them. Perhaps, with hindsight, you could have taken more care over the tender – but there will always be someone, eventually, who will underbid you. Perhaps you should have paid your staff larger salaries, but you know that your business could not support that and, indeed, the company that poached your staff may end up going to the wall anyway, because its outgoings were too high.

The human race is notoriously bad at learning from the mistakes of others. Everyone thinks that things are different for them. 'Well I know that X made that mistake and it cost him his company but if that had happened to me I would have known how to turn it to an advantage' – you know the sort of thing. It is ego talking, and not common sense. The most successful business people are the ones who watch and learn.

Running a business is a bit like driving. You may be a very good and careful driver but you will always have to worry about the idiot who decides to overtake you on a sharp bend. Absorbing the message in this chapter will enable you to avoid the most common pitfalls. While you can learn a lot from the mistakes of others, on a more positive note you can also learn a lot from their successes, which is tackled in the following chapter. You should also look closely at the way you do business. It is often possible to revolutionise the way you operate by improving upon existing systems. Chapter 4 gives advice on running your business more effectively.

Chapter 3

Learning from others

A company can derive enormous value from comparing its ethos, systems, products, services, management and other processes with those in other companies – which do not have to be in the same industry sectors. If a business has, say, a good quality control strategy (see page 62) its basic structure will work in any other business. Most successful businesses demonstrate the ability to inspire or motivate their staff by the way that management interacts with employees. This ability, which can be developed through education and training within a company, knows no industry boundaries. If you are able to learn from a company at close quarters, for example, using the benchmarking technique outlined below, this means assimilating another culture. If you are sensible you will copy those things that you admire and add them into your company's culture. Sometimes, what we learn from others cannot directly translate into our own working environment but can none the less give us an idea and help us to be creative and develop a positive ethos of our own.

Benchmarking

Many companies have adopted a process called 'benchmarking', whereby one company is compared to others by measuring about 80 business functions, including financial, management, production and general business excellence factors (excluding products and services). Information gathered is compared with the performance of thousands of other small to medium-sized businesses held in a central database and, when analysed by an experienced business consultant, can produce a dramatic and revealing picture of a company's strengths and weaknesses. The idea of benchmarking is not to copy other companies – what works for one may not translate exactly to another – but to observe, analyse and perhaps stimulate useful ideas.

Web sites on benchmarking around the world

American Productivity and Quality Centre and the International Benchmarking Clearing house *www.apqc.org*

British Quality Foundation *www.qualityfoundation.co.uk*

California Council for Quality and Service *www.ccqs.org*

European Company Benchmarking (hosted by Enterprise Ireland) *www.forbairt.ie/services/busdev/competitive/benchmarking*

European Foundation for Quality Management *www.efqm.org*

Global Benchmarking Network *www.globalbenchmarking.org*

The DTI's Small Business Service (SBS)★ has been running its Benchmark Index since 1996 and, to date, over 2,000 companies have taken part. The Benchmark Index does not cover all industrial sectors, geographical regions and company sizes but it does give a true reflection of key issues that are relevant to all SMEs up and down the UK. The Benchmark Index is managed and delivered on behalf of the SBS by Winning Moves Ltd.

The first step in the process is to register and fill in a questionnaire. This can be provided by the SBS or downloaded from its web site *www.benchmarkindex.com* (try the main DTI web site★ if you have trouble accessing the SBS site directly). From the start, the process requires the advice and support of a business adviser at the DTI, who will transmit your data to a secure database which then generates a Benchmark Index Report. This report provides comprehensive and quantifiable performance indicators, highlighting the company's strengths and weaknesses against the comparison group chosen. Businesses in the group are selected according to several factors – similar company size, production levels, numbers of staff, turnover and so on.

The Benchmark Index is divided into quartiles. After being analysed companies quickly find out whether they fit into the upper quartile (the most successful SMEs), the lower quartile (the companies that need to work hard to improve performance) or are somewhere in the middle two quartiles.

In the final stage of the process, improvement action plans are developed between the business adviser and the company and a time frame for implementation is selected.

It is difficult to give benchmarking costs, for two reasons. First, it depends how the process is packaged by the individual business advisers. Your company may simply need a three-day diagnostic exercise, or you may choose to have an ongoing programme of the full benchmarking process. Second, depending upon where your business is based in the UK, you could qualify for free or subsidised benchmarking. Businesses in areas of perceived economic need, called Objective 2 areas, may qualify for assistance. These areas are chosen by the government and constantly change, so you would need to check with the SBS to find out if you are in an Objective 2 area.

Benchmarking analysis

The Benchmark Index uses a series of measures in order to measure the financial and non-financial performance of participating companies.

Financial performance is split into three categories:

- sales and profit performance
- value creation
- asset management.

When assessing performance, advisers need to see all company accounts and financial material – either from inception, if the company is new, or for the last couple of years. The whole benchmarking procedure is confidential.

Non-financial performance covers:

- **customers** The size of the customer base, its relationship with the company, market research and marketing techniques
- **employees** Salary levels, training offered, promotion prospects, corporate culture, time management, flexible working practices, management skills etc.
- **suppliers** The company's relationship with suppliers, any networking technology, contracts and penalty clauses and so on

- **investment in the company** This covers all kinds of investment – financial and otherwise. Investment could be in training,
  research and development or product development
- **market growth and penetration** Has the company made the
  most of new markets, export markets, collaborative markets?
  Has it seized opportunities and, if so, how well has it done?

Benchmarking is supposed to be a regular exercise, not a one-off
procedure. Undergoing the analysis at regular intervals enables
companies to determine whether they have achieved the necessary
levels of improvement.

As well as providing insight into the performance of individual
companies, benchmarking also gives a general picture of business
practice – for better and worse. In a 1999 report called *Closing the
Gap,* generated jointly by the SBS, Cranfield University School of
Management and the University of Cambridge Judge Institute of
Management Studies, many 'eye-opening results' from the
Benchmark Index were cited:

- 25 per cent of companies are destroying the value of their businesses by not getting an adequate return on their capital
- if creditors called in their debts tomorrow, 25 per cent of the
  sample would go bust
- the bottom 25 per cent of companies are achieving profit levels
  that are one-tenth of those achieved by the top 25 per cent
- supplier performance is poor. Lower-quartile companies clearly
  do not have control over their suppliers as up to 75 per cent (by
  value) of the supplies they receive are delivered late
- overhead management is a key issue. The bottom 25 per cent of
  companies spend three times as much outlay on overheads as the
  top 25 per cent. They have three times the number of indirect
  employees and require twice as many managers per employee
- many companies invest more in marketing – claiming specific
  talents, resources or knowledge in that area – than they do in
  actually building up these capabilities. More money is spent on
  marketing, research and development than on training
- lower-quartile companies lose six days per year per employee
  through absenteeism. This is equivalent to a 500-person business losing 12 person years through absenteeism for every year
  worked

- well over half of the sample spent nothing on research and development. Even the upper-quartile performers spent on average a mere 0.7 per cent of their turnover on research and development
- the figures for training expenditure are even more disturbing. The average spend for upper-quartile performers is 0.5 per cent of turnover. The average for the sample as a whole is 0.2 per cent
- 25 per cent of the companies benchmarked did not generate any income from new customers, products or markets.

The benefits of benchmarking

The process can yield tangible results for the companies that undergo benchmarking.

The rubber compounds manufacturer

This company, in the north of England, employs 60 people. It underwent benchmarking to test the feelings that the management of the company had about its strengths and weaknesses. The Benchmark Index compared the company's data against other companies in the rubber, plastics and processing industries and the subsequent analysis and recommendations resulted in the following improvements:

- 50 per cent reduction in complaints per order
- 40 per cent reduction in absenteeism
- 60 per cent fall in material re-processing
- 15 per cent reduction in set-up times
- 22 per cent reduction in scrap rates
- 5 per cent reduction in energy costs.

Benchmarking shows that if a company employs and trains the right people, identifies and creates successful products and develops and streamlines effective processes, it can move into the top quartile of successful companies. Follow-up analyses by the advisers have shown that most companies are able to make some improvement to their positioning, and many make dramatic improvements after undergoing benchmarking. Most companies that participate continue to be benchmarked at regular intervals (say, annually) because it is an effective way of keeping their company up to scratch.

The leisure club

When a large club, with about 70 staff, opened in a regional city in the late 1990s it was the first of its size in that location. It prospered and gained nearly 4,000 members. The club – part of a national chain – was concerned that it needed to keep its customer base, so it underwent benchmarking. The process highlighted several areas that could be improved. Financial management needed to be tightened up and the company required an aggressive sales campaign. It was also necessary to train staff so that they could not only deal effectively with their routine tasks but also foster good customer relationships. Following these beneficial results the club intends to make benchmarking a regular procedure.

Benchmarking may seem, to the emerging business, a jargon-ridden exercise in juggling figures. But the authors of *Closing the Gap* have boiled it all down into an easily understandable key message: 'Keep delivering a great service to your customers, but continually look for ways of reducing the cost of delivering this service through the three key levers – overhead management, supplier management and people management'.

Ways of running your business more effectively are described in Chapter 4.

Other sources of learning

People like to apply labels to everything, and business gurus and consultants love to invent jargon. It helps to make their function more mysterious and their pronouncements more authoritative. In today's frenetic business world, it is common to summarise principles and processes using snappy terms that reflect the system they describe – for example, benchmarking. Jargon can be offputting (and sometimes explanations of business terminology can be bewildering) but behind all the buzz words there lurks basic common sense which, if translated and applied to the emerging SME, can be of genuine use in helping a business to re-invent itself, expand and consolidate its market position.

Terms such as 'mentors', 'e-possums' and 'incubators' proliferate in business literature and on the web sites of US business gurus. Don't be turned off by the jargon – the concepts they express can be useful.

Mentors

A successful entrepreneur may have certain gifts – creativity, marketing know-how, willingness to take risks and responsibility – but be weak in other areas such as accounting, human resource management or scientific and technical knowledge. Clear-thinking business people recognise when they are deficient in certain skills. In the past few years one of the most helpful ideas to take a hold in the business world has been mentoring – having someone who will act as a personal business trainer and coach you in all the aspects of business that you are uncertain about or in which you lack the necessary experience. A mentor can be from either inside or outside your company.

The Institute of Directors (IoD),* for example, has long recognised the need for owner/managers to network with others who have skills that complement their own. The IoD's array of services is geared towards allowing the owner/managers of SMEs to meet with and learn from others. The IoD department that deals with professional development acknowledges that 'owner/managers are often professionally lonely' and promotes networking strategies such as executive coaching and mentoring as a supplement to more obvious solutions such as reading relevant literature and attending trade events and training courses. The IoD runs an executive coaching scheme that matches enquiries from owner/managers to a pool of entrepreneurs whose credentials have been checked and who are happy to give the benefit of their experience and skills to others.

The most effective way of having a mentor 'on tap' is to appoint an experienced person as a non-executive director to your company. Many a retired business person has gone on to advise other companies for a few days a week. It is important to choose the right person – if he or she does not understand the business or the people, the end result could be worse than having no one at all. Someone who has a wealth of experience in your business arena but is no longer a competitor is ideal. Non-executive directors come cheaper than consultants or training courses. They can also, by mutual agreement, stay only as long as your need for learning.

Business Link★ advice units (see page 15) source mentors for emerging businesses, or you could make your own arrangement with someone that you know and respect. It is usual to treat mentors as non-executive directors and pay them a modest retainer for their time and expertise.

A more expensive and more permanent option is to select a partner or appoint a full-time company director who also has the necessary experience to act as a mentor. However, with this option you are taking on someone who will have much more of a say in running your company than a straightforward mentor (who should just advise you).

Many observers consider that the dotcom companies which crashed so spectacularly did so mainly because of youthful hubris, and that the protagonists would have been better advised to ally their techno-skills to old-economy mentors who could have provided the basic business skills that so many of them were lacking.

The food manufacturing company

In the early 1990s, a company was founded that specialised in making high-quality Asian breads for the supermarket chains. The founder recognised that he needed both a mentor and capital, so he approached a retired entrepreneur who had built a similar speciality food company before selling it to a larger conglomerate. The retired entrepreneur was willing to invest in the company in return for an equity stake, and became the company's non-executive chairman. More valuable than his money was his wealth of experience. He had succeeded in breaking into the marketplace at the gourmet end and in filtering a brand down into the public's consciousness until it became a mass-market product. The two men found that they had a perfect partnership. The younger man was able to concentrate on production matters while relying on the older man to pinpoint the best time to expand, move into new markets, create a new brand and invest in plant and equipment.

E-possums

This concept, which grew up in Australasia, describes the process whereby young techno-wizard employees teach senior old-guard management about the Internet – a kind of reverse mentoring.

The system, which involves the young teaching the not-so-young about technology, is successful on several levels. Firstly, providing the participants work well together, it is a fun way for technophobe directors and managers to learn about the Net's potential and drawbacks. The older staff do not lose face due to their lack of knowledge because they are already respected within the company for their superior expertise in other areas. Secondly, it is a cost- and time-effective way of training senior staff because there is no requirement to travel off-site and abandon business while being trained. E-possums can pass on their skills to others during lunch-breaks, after work or whenever it can be fitted in at the workplace. Thirdly, it can serve as a subtle method of training younger staff because, if the chemistry between the individuals is right, the older member of staff can teach the e-possum how to merge established business practices with new technology. A positive outcome would be to nurture a breed of future super-managers who have absorbed all the skills necessary to run a 21st-century business.

The international financial services company

A company selected a team of junior techno-wizard employees to be e-possums. The team spends a certain amount of time each week surfing the Net to find out about the latest developments in the industry and in technology, and gives a presentation to the board every month, explaining recent innovations to senior managers and directors and suggesting how they could be exploited by the company. This is combined with one-to-one technical tuition showing senior staff other ways of using the Net as a management tool – for research, information, e-banking and so on. The company has also set up a chat room resource on the company's intranet where learning and ideas are shared. Added to this, the e-possum team organises an annual training week to update all the company's staff on developments in IT and the Internet.

Incubators

These are organisations which exist to help businesses, and e-businesses in particular, to develop a business strategy and speed it quickly over whatever hurdles – for example, finance, technology development or recruitment – stand in the way of expansion.

Incubators have developed primarily to address what they see as the lucrative e-commerce market. They know how to develop a really good business plan, they can advise on working practices and company structure and they have the contacts to find funds. Although many of these high-powered incubators were created to deal with hi-tech start-up companies, there are other options in the more modest sections of the business arena.

Incubators exist in the guise of Business Link★ advice units, which provide advice and support (see page 15), venture capital firms (see page 131) and full-service incubators, many of which were formerly accountancy firms but now call themselves business consultants. All of these incubators have become wary of e-projects since the dotcom fiascos of 2000, when many of them lost a lot of money (both their own and some on behalf of investors). It is much harder to register with them now if you are a potential dotcom.

Some drawbacks exist. Many incubators have not been around long and many offer a limited service. They may be able to take a company only so far along the road because they have not built up a network of good contacts for funds, etc. Also, following the reappraisal of e-business by many financial institutions and investors which lost a lot of money through dotcom failures, many incubators find it much more difficult to raise finance for clients.

It is not impossible though. A full-service incubator is probably the best bet for any business because these companies have evolved from accountancy firms through management consultants and so have all the useful contacts in place. Full-service incubators are tougher on business ideas, for a start. They will deconstruct whatever idea you have and re-assemble it so that it really works, or they will tell you that it does not stand a chance – no false optimism is tolerated.

In a report published in autumn 2000 called *Getting Wealth in a Wired World*, PricewaterhouseCoopers list three requirements of a business-to-business incubator:

- the incubator should know your industry well
- select a full-service incubator with a history of working with high-tech and high-growth businesses
- go for a global incubator, with branches around the world, to help build an instant operation on an international scale. Perhaps there will be a regional phase in step one, but that may quickly need to become global.

To find out more, contact UK Business Incubation (UKBI)* for a list of incubators in the UK. Alternatively a Business Link, bank or business associate might be able to recommend an incubator.

Technology and knowledge transfer

Amongst the many services offered by the DTI is TCS (formerly known as the Teaching Company Scheme). This enables companies to take advantage of the wealth of scientific, engineering, technological and business management skills and knowledge available in universities and other research- and technology-based organisations (called 'knowledge bases' by the scheme).

Each TCS programme involves one or more high-quality graduates (known as associates) working in a company for two years on a project which is central to the company's needs. This enables the associates to benefit from industry-based training and promotes the sharing of technical and management skills. It is intended to encourage competition, develop future leaders and give businesses a strategic edge.

Support is available in the form of a DTI grant to the university or other establishment loaning the associate. An SME requesting help contributes about 40 per cent of the direct costs of the programme. The TCS annual report for 1998-9 reported that SMEs could expect, on completion of a programme, an average profit of £32,000 per associate and an average recurring annual profit increase of £125,000, leading to additional jobs and trained staff. Proposals can be submitted at any time by the knowledge bases in partnership with a UK-based company, but must be in a business sector or technology area covered by the 11 government departments and research councils which fund TCS. For more information, contact the Teaching Company Directorate (TCD),* which manages the scheme.

Skills acquisition and consolidation

This is training. In an era of change, it is essential that skills throughout a company are kept at the highest level. It is possible to import specialists but one can only do that for so long. Lack of in-house training and promotion from within can make a company extremely vulnerable if its key personnel are headhunted by other companies. No matter how much you think you know about business, it is vital to stay alert to learning possibilities, both for the employees in your company and your own self-development.

It is important to identify those skills which will be of genuine benefit to the company. Sometimes, the acquisition of management techniques can be to the detriment of a company rather than adding something, because they can bring a rigid orthodoxy to what was previously a successful flexible environment. It can be helpful to keep up with management theory by reading relevant books and publications, while bearing in mind that what works for one organisation may not work for another. In general, however, acquiring skills in your organisation can bring valuable benefits. By helping employees to develop their potential – whether this means brushing up their IT skills or sending them on industry training schemes – you are likely to improve productivity and communication within your company.

As in the case of benchmarking, it has become fashionable to learn from other companies directly rather than via academic means such as sitting in lectures and looking at overhead slides. A useful scheme in operation at the time of writing is a DTI venture called Inside UK Enterprise (IUKE),* which organises exchange visits between companies. It matches those who wish to learn new methods and techniques with a database of about 170 host companies, selected because they are outstanding in particular areas such as research and development, productivity, team working or corporate communication.

The scheme can greatly benefit companies that are in the process of growing and developing. The great value of real life – learning from someone who has been through it before you – rather than dry management theory, cannot be overestimated in the process of embracing change.

The specialist engineering company

This company entered into the IUKE scheme over two years ago and since then over 80 employees have been on approximately 40 one-day visits to major UK companies across a wide range of industries. The managing director reports that he sends a wide cross-section of people on these visits because it raises awareness, at all levels, of how other businesses are run. He believes that people think of ideas themselves after seeing others' successful practices, rather than through having systems imposed upon them in the workplace. The scheme has helped his company grow and adapt by noting the differing approaches of the host companies to benchmarking, performance targets, procurement strategies and cultural issues.

Other organisations that can offer information about skills acquisition and training include your local Business Link and the Local Enterprise Development Unit (LEDU)* in Northern Ireland. Enterprise Agencies are also a source of support (see page 16).

As well as learning from others, you must look closely at your own business to achieve the best results. The next chapter explains how to improve the internal structure of your organisation.

Chapter 4

Running your business more effectively

This chapter looks at how to streamline processes within your company and improve business relationships. It also explains how to foster an innovative working environment.

Knowledge management

The resources and accumulated experience of a company – people, skills, facts and figures, technology – are its greatest assets. By encouraging the sharing of information at all levels, you should be able to improve the productivity of your business.

The Artificial Intelligence Applications Institute at the University of Edinburgh, which, among other things, studies the applications of technology in the business world, defines knowledge management as the ability of an organisation to manipulate successfully intelligence about markets, products and technologies which can generate profit or add value to that business (described as 'knowledge assets'). As well as managing these assets, it is necessary to manage the processes which relate to them, which means developing, preserving and sharing knowledge in order to fulfil organisational objectives.

In other words, possessing bare facts alone is not enough – they must be analysed, used properly and disseminated throughout the organisation in order to provide the maximum benefit to your business. Encouraging employee involvement and listening to feedback so that existing procedures can be improved is important.

The development of the Internet means companies have access to more information than ever before. They can gather information about shifts in global markets very quickly and, through electronic data capture from their own customers, they can constantly review their own particular marketplace. A wide array of services and software exists to meet the modern craving for information on tap.

All of this has had a huge impact even on low-tech companies. Even the sole trader working from home making craft items finds himself relying on the Internet to communicate, source supplies and pay bills. The influence of the World Wide Web is discussed in Chapter 5.

Some business organisations are convinced that the 'old order' has to change. This school of thought suggests that for companies to be truly successful they have to forget the old hierarchies – the departmental ways of doing things, when each section of the company jealously hugged its own secrets to its chest and was suspicious of anything 'not invented here' (i.e. developed or initiated elsewhere within the organisation). Now, according to prevailing wisdom, companies have to 'flatten out' their structures. This means that traditional management roles and responsibilities become shared among teams of managers and workers, who use their shared knowledge and power to run systems within the company more effectively. Such *glasnost* is common among new-technology companies.

Knowledge has to be acquired, shared and stored so that all can have access to it. Sharing company knowledge can increase its value, as knowledge is a valuable resource. Whereas, once upon a time, companies' computer networks used to restrict access to information on a need-to-know basis, now it is considered vital that as much non-confidential information as possible is posted on businesses' intranet systems for all to digest and process, for the good of the company.

As with e-possums (see page 45), this trend points towards employees being creative and analytical – finding the information, adding it to the company's assets, analysing that information as to how it may best serve the company and sharing that knowledge with others in the organisation. It all suggests that in the 21st century employees are expected to be intelligent and not just 'process' information and perform tasks unthinkingly. Routine functions (and here we have the crux of the matter) can be delegated to sophisticated technology. So, for example, in the case of a company selling goods over the Internet, the basic business of retail could be done by e-tailing technology while humans could be better employed analysing the marketplace, looking for market gaps, discovering niche markets, spotting declines in markets, then feeding this information through to the company so that the e-tailing programs can be altered. (For more on the marketplace, see Chapter 6.)

Although they may seem to apply mostly to organisations involved in e-commerce, the principles of knowledge management are relevant to every small business. Knowledge management requires an organisation which has a respect for knowledge, therefore a respect for training, and which rewards creative employees who contribute to the company's value. It also requires a high degree of developed communication channels within a company.

The proponents of knowledge management theory say that even the most junior employees need to have a broad understanding of the business of their organisation and how their work fits into the overall scheme of things. All employees need to act in an entrepreneurial fashion by taking on a degree of responsibility and authority and show capability and intelligence.

In fact, this state of affairs exists in most small businesses which employ ten people or less. In a business this small it is impossible for anyone to just be a 'processor' (unless they are, say, a home worker for a manufacturing company). Everyone in a small company understands the business they are working for, adopts flexible roles, is able to take on more responsibility when required and can contribute to the creativity of the company. It is when a company grows that the initial teamwork can get lost as new people are brought in, more specialists appear and management processes become more cumbersome. The company that grows successfully in this century is likely to be one that retains the knowledge-sharing climate of its early years.

People management

British companies have a tendency to underestimate the value of the people they employ. They spend less on training than any other industrially and commercially developed country, are liable to scorn the building of corporate cultures and undertake quality control with cynicism. Many companies assume that a monthly pay cheque is enough motivation for most people. As the Benchmark Index showed, British companies spend a derisory amount on research and development (see page 41). And to top it all, a large number ignore employees as a valuable source of creative ideas.

Good people management involves identifying better ways that will help you to recruit and retain employees. (This means motivation, good supervision and training.) It is important to build a positive atmosphere and to broadcast the prevailing culture of your business to job applicants. You should also ensure that you know what employees are up to at all times.

Many employers forget that employees need to feel valued. People work well if they are praised. People work well if they understand fully what is expected of them. Therefore, if you communicate fully the quality control standards and other specifications that you wish staff to follow, train people how to manage the systems and then make sure everyone knows when someone has performed well, the results should be highly positive. Some companies choose to take things further and introduce an element of competition and reward – free tickets for two on Eurostar for the person with that month's best sales figures, for example. But incentives such as this are a double-edged sword. They can cause resentment because, perhaps, the same person keeps winning; or the scheme is run only for the benefit of income-generating departments and, say, the poor old accounts department is never included, even though its staff may contribute greatly to a healthy cashflow situation.

There are other ways to foster good relationships and ensure a productive workplace, some of them informal and involving social activities. Many companies follow the US example of organising outside work activities to encourage team spirit and good employer-employee relationships. These can take the form of regular sporting activities (a regular game of company rounders, perhaps management against staff or department against department); social activities such as company barbecues or dinner-dances; or they can take a more structured form with an element of training included such as the increasingly popular 'paint-balling' games where companies undertake structured team 'war games'.

For more on employee relations see Chapter 11.

Managing business relationships

Your relationships with customers, subcontractors, suppliers, agents and distributors and financial institutions need to be cultivated and strengthened as much as possible. This is probably the most difficult area to control and develop, since many business relationships are conducted at a distance and subject to some factors that are beyond your company's control. But these relationships are important. Your company is balanced, like a spider in the centre of its web. The web is intricate and delicate. If one part unravels, the whole business is in danger. Business relationships have to be constantly maintained to ensure that this silken network does not come apart.

Customers

Customer relationships are vital, but in some businesses, such as high-street retailing, interaction with clients has become sloppy. Many people feel that the interpersonal skills of sales assistants often leave much to be desired, as does their knowledge base. Where are the shop assistants who can tell a customer how to care for a particular garment? Where are the shop assistants in DIY stores who can tell a customer how to perform a particular repair task? How many high-street names (such as C&A and Marks & Spencer) have run into trouble by not researching customer needs or giving customers what they want and simply aiming for high profit margins? How many manufacturing companies are reactive instead of proactive when it comes to marketing their products?

Companies that do not conduct business over the Internet need to put their customer relationships under a microscope. They need to evaluate continuously the quality of service that they provide to customers. In this age of almost unlimited consumer choice in the developed world, customers can and do choose where they purchase and what that experience will be. The supermarkets that were forced to abandon loyalty cards (see page 102) have recognised that the customer is fickle and will be swayed by whatever he or she deems to be attractive that week – be it organic produce, buy-one-get-one-free, in-store crèches, in-store restaurants and so on. The buying experience has to be more than just a simple transaction.

Customers want named contacts, personal service, comprehensive information and quality products at a low cost. They demand these things. Ignore them at your peril.

It is important to appoint staff who can deal politely and effectively with customers, as these people represent your company to the public. You should also have in place a procedure for dealing with complaints:

- staff should be trained to handle whatever attitude a customer may display with courtesy and a positive attitude
- company policy on refunds or exchanges should be prominently displayed throughout the facility
- there should always be a written record of each complaint, preferably agreed and signed by the customer
- customer services staff should be monitored and assessed at frequent intervals
- staff should have name tags so that customers can identify them
- staff should also have clear instructions on how much decision-making is devolved to them and at what point they need to defer to management.

Internet customers

Due to the nature of e-commerce, companies trading online have additional responsibilities (see Chapter 5). Customer relationship management (CRM) has become big business ever since people started trading on the Internet – understandably so, since the customer is largely unseen and represents merely an electronic transaction on a screen. CRM software claims to improve the quality of service given to e-customers. A package can make a web site much easier for a customer to access and order from. It can also make a web site more interactive, allowing the customer to ask questions about a product that may not be answered on the site.

AMR Research Inc., a US consultancy, predicts that the e-business relationship management market will have grown from $4.4 billion in 1999 to $20.8 billion by 2004. In an article by Dave Caruso and Peggy Menconi called 'Success in the Internet World Requires a Great CRM Strategy', the authors cite the following as key considerations for managers preparing to implement customer-focused strategies in a business-to-business environment:

- organisations with CRM strategies realise that when customers buy products they implicitly buy into the way the vendor does business. Customers regard suppliers in total terms, taking into account the price and quality of the products, the flexibility of the company and how it uses technology to interact with the customer. They also want good financial terms, prompt delivery, product availability and ease of doing business
- customers want the vendor's web site or telephone system to offer pertinent information that is easy to access and helps them to meet their needs. They expect to speak to the right person immediately, and they expect that person to know about them and their needs
- call-centre agents must have transaction-related information at their fingertips. They must know who the caller is, his or her phone number, where he or she is located, and so on, not to mention what products the caller has purchased and which are under warranty. Agents should know about everything from pending sales to whether their CEO is visiting the customer's headquarters today.

To sum up, 360-degree corporate-wide knowledge is critical to success in a service-driven world.

It is interesting that the hi-tech world now seems to think that it has invented the concept of customer service. Perhaps this is because after being lost by so many old-economy companies, the concept was not passed on to the dotcom start-ups (whose downfall was partly due to bad customer relationships). The reason for the growth of CRM software is because so many people have become dissatisfied with e-tailing, its brusqueness and its failure to engage with the customer, by maintaining anonymity, in the face of the customer's needs.

Subcontractors

Occasionally a company sets out from the beginning to capture the business of one very large client. It may seem wonderful, at the outset, to have full and continuous employment for your workforce and to be dealing with a big company that presumably has no cash-flow problems and therefore pays on time, but this policy is in reality rather foolish.

Such security can very quickly evolve into dangerous insecurity. Total reliance upon one client means that if its patronage is withdrawn your business cannot survive. If you are in this type of situation, you should endeavour to enlarge your client base and provide your company with an escape route in the event that your one big client makes other arrangements – cuts back on orders, say, or changes its system of payment.

However, some companies that want to pursue this course of action may find they have painted themselves into a corner. Firstly, their resources may be stretched to capacity simply to cope with the work of that one client. Secondly, there may be a contractual obligation not to do any work at all for any other company in the same field. Thirdly, they may not be able to, or indeed wish, to expand their workforce to take on new business, even if they were able to generate any. Expansion which requires a large financial investment may not be advisable in any case. Any increase in overheads at this crucial point in development should be viewed with caution.

For many, the answer lies in phased expansion – subcontracting, engaging temporary staff, using freelances and employing home workers (see Chapter 11). Careful management of such expansion could result in the contracts being taken from a subcontractor at a later date and eventually brought in-house – the temporary staff becoming permanent, the freelances being offered permanent contracts, or the home workers being phased out. In this scenario any capital outlay will have been financed by the extra business gained.

The first decision to be made is whether you find the work first and then put the temporary staff in place, or the other way round. The answer depends upon the type of business you are in.

- If you are operating a consultancy you might be able to offer freelance consultants a percentage of profits if they generate some of the business themselves.
- If you are going after manufacturing contracts which you know will have very tight deadlines, your infrastructure should be in place before you pitch for business.
- Employing home workers on piecework (where you have to set them up with equipment and materials before they can start, and provide some training) requires a more structured plan, engaging workers in stages as contracts are procured.

- Subcontractors' contracts should prevent them, as far as possible, from stealing your existing customers.

Suppliers

It pays to search for ways in which the supply base of your company can be rationalised. As the trend towards outsourcing non-core business activities continues, the risk of a higher level of problems with suppliers increases.

In your relationship with suppliers, aim for the following:

- before finalising any outsourcing contract, work out a service level agreement to which costings are linked
- specifications should be adhered to, with anything below par to be unacceptable
- delivery dates should be met and quantities supplied must be correct; agreements should contain penalty clauses
- your suppliers should have the same quality control mechanisms as your own company
- suppliers' computerised ordering systems should be flexible enough to be changed if they do not suit your operations
- your suppliers should be contactable at all times in order to sort out any problems that may occur
- if you have a computer-based ordering system linked to a central warehouse, you need to know that the suppliers are updating the system constantly
- before you know that a supplier is reliable and always delivers on whatever date you select, it is advisable to bring orders forward to ensure that you are not kept waiting. Once you are sure that a supplier is dependable you can adjust the timescale.

In short, your relationship with your suppliers needs to be based on trust and good communication. This means careful selection at the outset. Do not sacrifice the advantages of the attributes mentioned above in favour of a cheaper price. You will lose any financial advantage very quickly through a supplier's poor performance.

Note that entrusting key activities to suppliers can be risky. If you put your credit control in the hands of another company that does not pursue debtors with the same urgency that your own company would, it affects your cashflow, not the other company's.

Regular contact between nominated members of staff should be set up. Frequent changes of staff responsible for contact with suppliers is irritating and unnerving for the supplier. He or she wants to deal with someone who is familiar at all times with the business being transacted. Similarly, your company representative wants to deal with a familiar and knowledgeable person at the other end, with at least one fallback in the event of that person's absence. When technological communication fails, because the computer system is down, someone needs to be able to pick up the phone and say 'I'll speak to Mary. She'll sort this out.'

Some very large companies actually train their suppliers to supply a quality service in line with the ethos of the purchasing company (to meet standards over and above safety regulations, for example). SMEs rarely have that luxury but there is nothing to stop the management of a small purchasing company working with key personnel from the supply company to devise a system of controls and administration that makes everyone happy.

Increasingly, companies are networking their computer systems to other companies' to share knowledge and make functions more streamlined. This can be done through third parties, such as banks, so that financial transactions can be processed more effectively (see Chapter 7). Alternatively, those companies that outsource their peripheral activities, such as warehousing or logistics, might network through a logistics company which serves as a conduit of information for both the core company and the suppliers.

Agents and distributors

Your ideal, as discussed earlier in the section on knowledge management, is for agents and distributors to be more than just 'processors' – you want them to share knowledge, to be innovative, creative and to recognise opportunities. Agents and distributors should be, in part, your company's eyes and ears in the marketplace – especially if it is an overseas market. An agent who does not supply you with continuous market information is not doing his or her job. He or she should be able to spot business opportunities in the home market and relay them back to you. Many an exporting venture has foundered on the lack of ambition of an agent. For more on overseas agents see page 101.

The property agent

A thriving estate agency decided to branch out into overseas holiday property and set up an alliance with an estate agent in southern Spain. The Spanish agent's job was to identify properties that would be suitable for sale to British tourists and relay the information to the UK agent. For the first year this process ticked over, then the Spanish agent spotted a market need, which he transmitted to the UK. Many British buyers were having difficulty equipping their holiday homes in Spain, so he proposed that the two agencies between them should offer the complete package of a fully furnished home (decorated and equipped by the Spanish agent). This idea was tested and to the delight of both parties proved to be successful, enabling them to win out over the competition by removing this particular headache for holiday-home buyers.

Banks and financial institutions

Alas, business banking has changed. The days of the bank manager who gave his business customers a personal service have long gone. Now banks are trying to coax customers into electronic transactions and online banking. SMEs are being forced to do business by electronic means and charged for every cheque they pass through the banking system. Employees of financial institutions are rewarded for how many financial services they sell, not for how good a personal service they offer to customers. Nowadays many business relationships with banks and building societies are conducted with a copy of the Banking Code in one hand and the telephone number of a bank charges auditor in your pocket. However, banks made some positive moves during the 1990s to assist the business community. It is not all doom and gloom. For more about dealing with banks and other financial institutions, see Chapter 7.

Strategic alliances

Strategic alliances are relationships between two or more companies with complementary businesses, products or services that allow them to penetrate jointly a specific market by offering a greater range of goods or services. For example, in spring 2001 the hamburger giant McDonald's purchased a stake in Pret à Manger prior to the sandwich chain's expansion into the USA, making future consolidation of its share possible and allowing the latter to benefit from its longstanding US presence when locating outlets.

An alliance has to be based on mutual trust, aims, objectives and standards. Any partnership has to be worked at; communication has to be good. The most productive alliances share information successfully. Sometimes strategic alliances result in mergers or takeovers.

Stephen Graham, Vice President of the Global Software Partnering and Alliances Group of IDC, has outlined the following characteristics of successful strategic alliances:

- the same long-range vision and objectives
- a vested interest in the success of other alliance members
- the leverage to increase worldwide market share and gain or maintain a competitive advantage
- the creation of additional value for each alliance member and their customers.

Although his comments were particular to technology companies, they are relevant to any form of strategic alliance between organisations in any sphere of business. Another key factor in the success of such relationships is the presence of a mediator, to act as an independent voice and help decision-making.

It is common practice in the US to use an independent investment banker or specialist arbitrator to manage the negotiations between companies, as it has been known for lawyers to rack up huge bills by prolonging the negotiations. A good mediator can get things done and dusted in the shortest possible time. You should aim to find someone with specialist knowledge of your industry so that he or she can manage the negotiations effectively. The Chartered Institute of Arbitrators* can provide a list of members for any company looking for independent arbitration in business negotiations.

Maintaining standards and cutting costs

It is important to communicate your quality control standards throughout the organisation so that the business functions efficiently, and to implement cost-saving measures wherever the opportunity exists.

Quality control

The key to successfully managing the generation of new business through a phased expansion is quality control. The quality of products or services created by in-house staff is more easily monitored. Products or services created at a distance need more management time and effort to ensure that they maintain the standard already set by your company.

The first step in setting a standard by which subcontractors, temporary staff or homeworkers can operate is to set your requirements down in black and white. The document that sets out your standards would have to be agreed by the other party before any contracts could be drawn up. The second step is to make sure that it is understood – and this means a certain amount of training or induction into your company's standards and working practices.

If you are in a manufacturing business it may be that your clients set the standards. Some companies require that SMEs have the ISO 9000 quality award before allowing them to quote for work, and large retail companies often produce extensive manuals which outline the standard of goods they expect to be manufactured for them. Anything that falls below those standards will not be purchased and the manufacturing company will, eventually, lose the contract if a certain percentage of goods is found to be persistently below the required standard.

However, there is no harm in setting your own standards, for the benefit of all those that work for you. Service companies will probably not have quality requirements handed to them by clients, particularly if they are in a nebulous field such as consultancy where, often, the client does not know what he or she wants, let alone how to measure it. The answer is to decide in advance what it is that you want from your temporary employees, contractors and freelances. How are you going to ensure that they understand your requirements and how are you going to manage this new limb of your business operations?

Concentrate on:

- quality standards
- methods of operation
- training needs, and
- quality control management.

Many companies choose to put together a quality control handbook for staff. If you do this, it will need to be supported by training sessions, reporting sessions and regular updates of information. Quality control should not be about penalising people, but about encouraging them. The Japanese, the Germans and the Americans know how to encourage people and, consequently, implement good systems. Motivation, incentives and rewards are the key drivers for staff (see 'People management', on page 52).

Overhead management

This means ensuring that you do not allow your company's overhead costs to grow unnecessarily. For some businesses, such as those in the media, glamorous city-centre offices with designer furniture and modern art on the walls may be justifiable, because image matters a great deal in this sector. For other types of business, especially in areas to which the public is admitted, conspicuous expenditure is unnecessary.

Burdening a business with a costly image, too many highly paid managers who do not generate income, crippling rents and rates, the latest technology which does not pay for itself or add any value to your business and so on, is a recipe for failure. Even a prudently run company, which does not have expensive overheads, can look for any fat to be trimmed off.

Introducing different ways of working may result in savings (see page 88). Energy audits can sometimes result in large savings on overheads. Just paying someone to do a tariff audit (look at your energy bill) can result in a challenge to your energy supplier or a change of supplier, enabling you to make significant savings. A corporate culture of energy-saving (ensuring that employees do not leave lights or computers switched on, and so on) can cut energy bills.

Building an innovative company

During 2000 a joint study between the Design Council and the DTI called *Living Innovation* looked at what lies behind 1,000 of the most innovative products and services developed in Britain since the mid-1990s. The study concluded that the most innovative companies tend to:

- inspire their employees
- encourage creativity (i.e. employers are flexible about implementing ideas and listen to both employees and customers with an open mind), and
- have close connections with customers.

The report can be downloaded from *www.livinginnovation.org*

The Design Council recommended that companies stick to the three rules of innovation – *inspire, create, connect*. In other words, to be successful you must develop a corporate atmosphere of creativity and be open to change. You must encourage your staff to have ideas and to communicate them. You must encourage your managers to be receptive and analytical. You must encourage your customers to communicate their wants and needs.

'Inspire'

A company's leader or leaders need to create a climate of trust and co-operation with their employees. If people feel they are supported they will respond by having the confidence to make constructive criticisms, offer suggestions for improvement and be creative.

The helmet maker

A one-man surfboard manufacturer developed an idea for a helmet which would reduce loss of heat from the head and allow surfers to surf for longer in the season when the water was much colder. A local lifeboat crewmember also suggested that the helmet could be worn by RNLI members. The RNLI was very demanding in its requirements, because of the importance of safety in all its equipment, and other companies were offered the chance to develop the helmet. However, the one-man company, with the aid of advice from the local Business Link (and a design award that enabled him to raise funds), finally won out over the competition and won the RNLI contract, making special adjustments to the helmet design as a result of RNLI recommendations. The one-man company is now a five-person manufacturing company which has been developed purely because one man listened intently to his customers and had the tenacity to follow through his idea despite the obstacles.

To take that one step further is to be an aggressively proactive company, where employees know that the company expects everyone to contribute constantly to the creative output of the company, to take risks and to problem-solve.

As the *Living Innovation* report says: 'Within "Living Innovation" companies, there is a significant devolution of responsibility, down the management chain, opening up opportunities for individuality. They tend to develop their people by mentoring, supporting them throughout . . . They go to great lengths to support, encourage, thank and reward their team and to celebrate success.'

'Create'

Innovative companies are strong advocates of teamwork – not just within the company but with those connected to the company, such as suppliers, partners and customers, who can all contribute to the creative process. Again, this means a receptive corporate culture, where customers and suppliers feel that they can have a productive dialogue with anyone they deal with in the company.

Innovative companies develop a 'hands-ready' policy amongst their managers. In other words, the managers are not 'hands-on' – driving projects on a day-to-day basis and making all the key decisions themselves – nor are they 'hands-off', leaving others to do the work. The top managers are there, fully informed about every step of a project, and able to assist when support is needed and problem-solve at crucial stages. The rest of the team feel that they have the freedom and power to get on with the job but have support and commitment from top management should help be required.

Increasingly, new companies prefer to blur the boundaries between management and employees. This is certainly the case in new technology driven companies with a high level of creativity, such as software houses or dotcoms, where management are fully engaged with all aspects of the business rather than setting themselves apart and being perceived as occupying a policy-making role.

The exact role which management plays is almost entirely dependent upon the type of business undertaken. Although an Internet entrepreneur might muck in with other employees, in a manufacturing set-up it may not be appropriate for the managers to join the workers on the production line. In fact it may be seen as intervention, and in this context would be unlikely to contribute towards a productive relationship. A lack of flexibility is more likely in rigidly hierarchical organisations where roles are clearly defined.

'Connect'

This refers to communication with customers and with the marketplace. Rather than impose new ideas, products or services on an existing customer base, it is vital to understand first what the marketplace needs and come up with the goods in light of that understanding. Sometimes, it is not the product or service which needs changing; it could be the way that a company accesses the marketplace, and it may mean that it needs to alter its distribution channels or business processes.

The aerospace systems developer

An aerospace systems company developing a silicon gyroscope demonstrated the benefits of networking and creative teamwork. It took advice from three universities on various aspects of the project, formed a partnership for fundamental research, found a manufacturing partner with the expertise necessary to develop the product and employed the services of a marketing consultancy. The marketing consultancy found that the potential marketplace would not recognise a supplier that came from the aerospace industry so it recommended that the company change its access to the marketplace and its distribution channels. This involved setting up a subsidiary company to access new distributors.

Also crucial is an understanding of where your company and its products or services stand in relation to the competition. Innovative companies tend to compete by emphasising quality, design and service rather than cost. An emphasis on quality can be particularly important when tackling overseas markets. The Design Council reminds everyone in its report that Britain is the only country that has recognised specifications and approval processes in place. The British Standards Institute (BSI)★ and the work that it does is highly regarded all over the world. Achieving BSI approval is a relatively lengthy procedure, requiring the submission of technical specifications and the rigorous inspection of products by BSI-appointed specialists, but most successful companies with overseas markets recognise the fact that making the extra effort to achieve BSI approval for their products is highly beneficial.

Understanding and respecting the customer and the marketplace will put your business on the right path to success. For more information see Chapter 6.

Focusing on what matters to you

There are many ways in which a developing company can get an edge over the competition and drive itself forward in a way that will maximise success without minimising quality. Just a few ideas have been touched upon in this chapter. It is possible to be blinded, or overwhelmed, by all the methodologies, schemes, philosophies and business practices that seem to be the 'flavour of the month'. It comes down to this: it is your company and, in the end, you need to make the decision about which route you want to take to drive your business forward.

Chapter 5

Using e-commerce and technology

Pressure to embrace new technology can add to the confusion for SMEs at this crucial stage of development. The implication, via the media and IT providers eager to sell their services, is that if you do not engage in e-commerce right now, you will be left behind and your business will die through lack of investment in innovation. Such messages tend to inject panic into an already stressful situation.

If you find the area confusing, you are not alone. Judging by the proliferation of articles in the business press about the basics of e-commerce and the findings of surveys conducted by various business organisations, a large percentage of the business community is still baffled by the rapid explosion of technology. The reality is that new developments offer as many pitfalls as positives, but if used wisely and appropriately technology can boost your business, enabling you to run it more effectively and reach new markets.

What is e-commerce?

'E-commerce' has been identified by the European Union's Information Society Directorate-General as 'any form of business transaction in which the parties interact electronically rather than by physical exchanges or direct physical contact'. The report suggests that the technology available has transformed modern business by enabling increased global competition, allowing easy access to overseas marketplaces and dramatically improving supply capabilities. These developments have led to increased customer expectations, and also to businesses demanding more of their supply chain partners.

The report goes on to emphasise that e-commerce is technology for change, and those companies that fail to embrace it wholeheartedly and regard it merely as an 'add-on' to their existing ways of doing business will gain only limited benefit. This view is one that many people would take issue with. The failure rate of many dot-com companies – operating solely under the banner of white-hot technology – would seem to be a testament to the fact that many solid 'old-fashioned' business practices need to underpin e-commerce.

There are four types of e-commerce:

- business-to-consumer (B2C)
- business-to-business (B2B)
- business-to-administration (B2A)
- consumer-to-administration (C2A).

Business-to-consumer

The type of e-commerce that attracts the big headlines is business-to-consumer, which is basically electronic retailing. This area has seen some outstanding successes and spectacular failures.

The Internet offers many advantages for small businesses. Business-to-consumer e-commerce allows companies to market overseas with relative ease. After all, on the Internet, providing you have placed your web site with the right search engines, the customer comes to look for you. You do not have to use an overseas agent to find customers (see page 101). Marketing overseas via the Internet is easier for British and American companies because English has become the agreed language of business on the Net. Credit-card transactions in theory remove the problem of dealing with transactions in foreign currencies. And, if you use a one-stop shop service like that offered by some Internet service providers and application service providers (see page 71), an external company will administer the entire actual sales procedure in return for a monthly subscription. Virginbiz.net currently charges between £80 and £200 for such a service.

It is said that you can buy anything on the Internet. However, buying and selling online can be fraught with difficulties. There have been problems with the security of credit-card transactions, supplies not meeting demand, slow delivery times and poor quality of goods. One of the biggest problems with the Internet is that businesses cannot really assess the size of the market or level of interest among Internet users until they have launched their own web site. For information and advice on how to go about this, see page 79. The section entitled 'Selling on the Internet', (page 76), looks at selling and marketing products online in more detail.

The barcode printing firm

A company in the north of England that specialised in printing barcodes was lagging behind the competition and business was slack when a young computer whizz-kid was taken on for a two-week work experience placement. In that short space of time he revolutionised the company's marketing strategy, launching the business into the world of e-commerce by setting up a web site. Within weeks the company had received an order from the USA worth $100,000 to provide barcode tags in several major airports. The company expects to net more than $1m from the Internet-based ordering system that the young man set up.

Business-to-business

This sector of e-commerce has been successful without all the attendant media hype. Studies done in the USA by AMR Research predict that business-to-business e-commerce will become a $5.7 trillion market by 2004, with many companies doing 60–100 per cent of their business online.

Business-to-business means business between businesses. This includes companies that supply other businesses with products, or businesses that buy from others. This can range from supermarkets ordering from suppliers, to banks making payments, to companies that provide office stationery on the Internet. Business-to-business e-commerce can be done on the World Wide Web or through a private intranet (an internal communication network which uses Internet software).

Auctions and clearing houses are becoming more important as suppliers compete to enter this field. Your company will need compatible IT systems in order to join the supply chain or bidding ring.

Recruitment agencies

The recruitment business has found a happy home on the Internet – particularly the business of supplying temporary staff. Traditional agencies sometimes do not bother to interview and select the temps first, although clients are often led to believe they are paying for this service. An Internet-based agency operates a bit like computer dating. Clients ask for temps with particular skills, and the agency will select the relevant people from their database so the customer can look at their CVs online. Once they have been selected, the temps can look at the company's details over the Internet before accepting the placement. Everyone is able to make mutually beneficial choices, very quickly, at less cost than using a traditional agency.

One of the most beneficial uses of the Internet for SMEs has been in procurement of supplies and equipment. A hosted digital marketplace is an interactive web site where the 'host' allows suppliers to offer their goods for sale to the companies who are members of that marketplace. The suppliers are allowed to do this on the understanding that they treat all the small member companies as though they were one large company and discount the goods accordingly. Participating members can therefore make considerable savings. Speaking at the launch of Elcom.com's new hosted digital marketplace early in 2000, the industry guru Sir John Harvey-Jones said, 'It's particularly vital for SMEs to use digital marketplaces to create a level playing field because individually they don't have much corporate spending clout over their suppliers.'

Basic office supplies can account for up to 60 per cent of total corporate expenditure and hosted digital marketplaces can reduce the amount spent on products by as much as 80 per cent. Sir John Harvey-Jones thinks that SMEs should go further and use e-commerce to deal with all the administration of a business. 'To compete, you must concentrate on the things that bring home the bacon, and outsource the rest. This is the only way that companies will survive in the global digital marketplace.'

It can be a good idea to use an application service provider (ASP) company to perform most company administration requirements –

credit control, invoicing, banking, procurement, payroll, sales – and so on. This option is quite appealing for a small company that needs to concentrate on producing the goods and services and cannot afford to employ full-time staff to do the admin work, but the costs need careful checking first.

Business-to-administration

This area has yet to develop fully but it basically covers all trans-actions/communications between businesses and government or other official organisations, such as trade associations and professional bodies. In the USA government departments are beginning to develop systems that will offer businesses the opportunity to make tax and social security payments by electronic interchange. In the UK, government departments are already putting most of their business information on web sites so that SMEs can have instant access to information, current regulations, forms and publications. The DTI says that downloading from its various web pages has largely replaced postal transmission of information, and this method enables people to avoid spending a long time on the telephone trying to find out basic information (see box opposite).

Consumer-to-administration

This expression means communications between the public and the government or other official organisations. Again, this is confined largely to the provision of information, regulations, forms and publications. Technically speaking, the government has been using electronic interchange for some time – paying benefits directly into individuals' bank accounts, for example. And it is a matter of course, nowadays, to instruct your online bank to transfer sums to the Inland Revenue (IR) or other government organisation. It is possible to email a growing number of completed forms to government departments – for example, tax forms to the IR.

What e-commerce can do for you

Entry into the global electronic marketplace has undoubtedly revitalised many companies by creating entirely new markets, redefining markets or just making supplies more obtainable and deliveries faster. (For more information, see 'Selling on the

Internet', page 76.) The trend looks set to continue: analysts expect that in the next few years a quarter of all customer contact will occur online.

It is becoming increasingly difficult to avoid e-commerce now that it impacts upon such a large number of business activities. For example, even a one-man company hand-crafting pieces of wooden

---

Links from the DTI web site

The DTI web site* has proved to be a huge boon to many small and new businesses. Here are just some of the organisations and information sites you can transfer to by clicking on the relevant link:

- Small Business Service (SBS)*
- The SBS Small Firms Loan Guarantee Scheme
- The SBS Smart Scheme (grants for research and development)
- National Federation of Enterprise Agencies*
- Business Links* in England, Small Business Gateway* and Business Information Source* in Scotland, Business Connect* in Wales, and EDnet* (the Economic Development Network for Northern Ireland)
- The Prince's Trust*
- Shell LiveWIRE* (sponsored by Shell UK)
- New Deal Initiative (for those moving into self-employment)
- The Phoenix Fund* (encourages entrepreneurship in disadvantaged communities and groups)
- Ethnic Minority Ministerial Forum
- UK Business Incubation (UKBI)*
- UK Science Park Association (UKSPA)*
- UK Online for Business
- The Trade Partners Export Awards for Smaller Businesses
- European Structural Funds
- Training and Enterprise Councils.

Additional links are in place to organisations that can help you improve your business performance and expand your company, or provide help with innovation and technology, rules and regulations, doing business in Europe and trade associations.

---

furniture in the Highlands of Scotland may find that his regular supplier of wood is online and prefers to take orders and payment over the Internet. His bank is probably putting pressure on him to take payment for his work only by credit card since electronic transfers are more convenient and safer than processing cheques. If he has sold a piece of work and wants to arrange delivery to a customer somewhere in the UK and his delivery service is computerised, this means that any consignment can be tracked from one end of the country to the other, every hour of the day, by information relayed by the driver from his WAP phone.

As outlined above, a big advantage of the electronic revolution is that marketing, sales, procurement, administration and financial dealings can all speedily be dealt with by someone else while your company concentrates on its core activity and simply monitors the e-commerce aspects.

Probably the greatest advantage of e-commerce is for those who trade in data and information-based products that can be delivered directly through the network (images, voice, text, software, ideas and publications). Everything can be done instantly. The customer can view the products, select one, pay and take delivery by downloading. It has totally changed some industries – for example, software houses. However, it has not had such impact on others.

It was predicted in 1999 that book publishing would die when the Internet began to offer literature that could be downloaded. This ignored the fact that the public like books because they are portable, need no power source, and beat reading text off a computer screen. The bestselling author Stephen King underestimated the appeal of the printed page, abandoning his Internet serialisation of a novel because the public lost interest (and was reluctant to pay for the instalments).

The specific business benefits of e-commerce are, in the view of the EU Information Society Directorate-General:

- reduced advertising costs
- reduced delivery costs (notably for goods that can be delivered electronically)
- reduced design and manufacturing costs
- improved market intelligence and strategic planning
- more opportunity for niche marketing

- equal access to markets (i.e. for SMEs vis-à-vis large corporations)
- access to new markets
- customer involvement in product and service innovation.

Britain on the Internet

In 2000 Which? Online published a survey in association with MORI which set out to identify trends in Internet usage and gauge public attitudes towards the Web and e-commerce. The good news for businesses is that the number of people getting hooked up continues to grow. Lower connection costs or free access, digital television and WAP phones have opened up the Internet to greater numbers of people, including less affluent groups. The survey provided the following profile of users and their purchasing power:

- almost 13 million people in Britain use the Internet
- more men use the Internet than women (61 per cent to 39 per cent), but women are signing up in greater numbers
- one in ten over-55s are 'silver surfers'
- 23 per cent of users regularly buy goods on the Internet, compared to 10 per cent in 1999
- among those who shop online, one in four men have bought a significant purchase, such as a holiday or computer equipment, compared with one in ten women
- popular purchases include books (23 per cent); CDs/videos (19 per cent); flights/holidays (19 per cent); computer software/hardware (19 per cent); cinema/theatre tickets (10 per cent); financial services (8 per cent); and groceries (6 per cent).

In spite of the rush to get online, a significant level of caution and scepticism remains among the public. Fifteen million people intend 'never' to get connected to the Internet, and among those who shopped online, only 11 per cent thought that customer service was better than on the high street.

Perhaps the greatest benefit of e-commerce is *information*. It is possible to do extensive and thorough research on markets, countries, other companies, regulations, government guidelines, institutions, statistics and much, much more without ever leaving your desk or employing someone to do it for you. The Internet effectively provides access to one huge database. A variety of software solutions and online 'sorters' have sprung up to meet the requirements of people to sift and filter through this information overload.

Selling on the Internet

This section discusses the pros and cons of using e-commerce techniques to sell products or services online. It can be read in conjunction with Chapter 6, which discusses how to improve a marketing strategy. For many businesses, the quick route to jumping on the technological bandwagon is to set up a web site promoting the company and selling its products (see page 79) – although this has to be properly promoted if the idea is to succeed. Many dotcoms failed to match sales to their marketing spend and were driven into liquidation.

The need to keep pace

The Internet is fast and furious. According to a 1999 *Sunday Times* special report on e-commerce, 'every piece of research done into the habits and predilections of web shoppers indicates that they want immediate fulfilment when they see something that they want'. Afam Edozie, marketing director of Virginbiz.net, an ISP, is quoted as saying: 'People expect instant gratification on the Net. When they reach your site they expect to be able to transact online that instant. With the exception of business-to-business e-commerce, they don't expect to receive an invoice or deal with cheques. They want delivery next day or, if the delivery companies can get their act together in the next few months, same-day delivery.' Achieving that level of service is a frightening thought for most developing SMEs. The development of customer relationship management (CRM) software reflects the need to meet Internet customers' particular needs (see page 55).

It can be difficult for a business to anticipate the level of demand for a product prior to going online, especially in a global market where customers' tastes are unpredictable (See 'Finding new markets abroad', page 99). Imagine that you are a manufacturer of model trains – high-quality models, the kind that are bought by adult collectors. Until now your well-organised little factory of six employees has had a modest success selling to a niche market in the UK via specialist publications. You start to advertise on the Internet and suddenly 30,000 orders come in overnight from the USA, Canada and Australia. You have promised delivery within 28 days and have taken customers' money, instantly, through electronic payment methods. Now you are in big trouble. You cannot set up a sub-contractor in time. You cannot train new staff in time. Orders keep coming in. You got into difficulty because you failed to think it all through before going online.

It is therefore vital to plan for change. Having a firm grasp of the potential as well as the limitations of your business is essential. You could invest in software which outlines different sales scenarios (such as Microsoft 'Project') to help you predict outcomes.

Businesses that are more at home online

E-commerce has proved of greater benefit to some types of industry than others. For example, companies that sell products such as holidays have profited from the technological revolution. These new direct travel companies set up packages with resorts around the world and then aim to fill their quota. Removing the 'middle-man' travel agent allows the customer to buy cheaper holidays. There are other attractions for consumers, too. They can browse through the holidays available online, rather than collecting brochures from the high street, and if they like a particular package they can find out instantly whether it is available on the relevant dates.

E-commerce has worked well for airlines too. Many companies offer special low-cost deals on 'last-minute' flights via the Internet which can be snapped up by discriminating surfers. Mostly, these are the 'grey' market (retired people with flexible time and good levels of disposable income). The consumer gets a good deal and the airlines fill what would otherwise be half-empty aeroplanes.

Companies that sell other companies' products through a themed catalogue on the Internet (for example, outdoor adventure wear), are likely to fare better than small manufacturers because they have a greater supplier base and, should one supplier let them down, they can probably source a similar supplier fairly quickly.

A sudden deluge of orders over the Internet could be a disaster if you were the model-train manufacturer described above. However, some companies can cope with a sudden upturn in fortune – for example, manufacturers with the capacity to process a lot of orders (such as those with large factories and an under-used workforce).

By carrying out research to establish the nature of your customer base and ensuring that your web site and marketing strategies are carefully targeted, you can maximise the chances of your company making an impact on the Web. You should also make sure that effective systems are in place to meet manufacturing, supply and delivery requirements (see Chapter 4).

The future of online shopping

Owner/managers need to think carefully about selling via the Net. A Which? Online survey (see page 75) identified resistance to e-commerce, and there are signs that the public is becoming disenchanted with the Internet. The majority of people in Britain in the year 2000 were not on the Internet at home. They may be on the Internet at their place of work but, if you are trying to sell personal consumer items or domestic services, employees are unlikely to be able to surf the Net to look for your web site. Regulations came into force in October 2000 which allow employers to monitor employees' personal use of telecommunications and computer time. After six months there had been some very high-profile sackings, suspensions and tribunals (see page 179).

The statistics regarding Internet use do not look very promising. For example, recent surveys have shown that only 36 per cent of British workers use the Internet each day – compared to 71 per cent of Americans and 45 per cent of Germans. Only about 14 million people use the Internet at home. Slow downloading times and expense are the major turn-offs to UK customers. So if you are selling products or services to a purely British market, investing in the World Wide Web may be an unnecessary diversion at the moment.

Perhaps the lucrative American market is what you should go for – or not. At the very end of 2000 a survey was published by the USA Economic and Social Research Council which reported that 28 million Americans had stopped using the Internet – an enormous decline for any marketplace. This dissatisfaction is said to have stemmed from frustration at not finding web sites, disenchantment with services such as e-banking and annoyance at poor delivery of goods. Many firms are able to deliver only during the day, when a lot of people are at work.

The situation has been so bleak for Internet companies that several have commissioned surveys to find out whether e-tailing (selling on the Net) is likely to take an upturn in 2001-2 before many of them go under. A survey conducted by Egg Internet Bank and MORI in late 2000 offered a possible ray of hope. It suggested that more than 23 million people in Britain could be online in the next 12 months – roughly half the population. One in ten people surveyed said that they planned to surf the Net, use email or switch on digital TV or a desktop computer for the first time. However, potential e-tailers should treat the findings with a pinch of salt. The survey seems to be based on 'possibles' not 'definites'. For example, 27 per cent of people said they would 'probably' vote via the Internet in the next General Election and 19 per cent said they would vote via digital TV (assuming they had the hardware). Thirty per cent said that they would be happy to bank online or buy insurance or a mortgage, but thought this would happen in the next four to five years.

For most companies that sell products to the ordinary consumer, Christmas is the time when the chickens come home to roost. Sadly, this was not the case with those companies that market solely through the Internet. The retail consultancy Verdict pronounced that Internet sales accounted for no more than 1 per cent of Christmas 2000 spending in the UK. The US-based company eToys was forced to admit that it sold only half the amount of products it expected to in the run-up to Christmas and would be drained of cash by March 2001 unless things drastically changed.

Setting up a web site for e-commerce

When planning a web site, look at your competitors' sites. Spend an hour or two surfing them and work out what you could do better. Think about who would visit your site and what you want them to use your site for – simply contact details and information? Or to purchase your products? Graphics matter because they create an immediate impact. Ensure that the pictures you use, whether photographs or downloaded images from the Net, are of a high quality and appropriately sized and cropped. Check the text for your site before settling on a final version. It is a good idea to type it on a word-processor so that it can be spell-checked first.

When designing a web site aim for clarity rather than clutter, and bear in mind the following tips:

- include an informative home (opening) page, which tells the user everything about your business and provides links to other pages. Try to make it represent your company image. You could start off by posting a brief explanation of the products or services you offer alongside an introductory visual and/or the logo of your company
- put in place a contacts page with your email, address, fax and telephone numbers. Your customers are more likely to take up your service if you are easily contactable
- graphics or visuals on your site make the downloading process very slow. If you use too many of them on your home page, users will get frustrated and exit before the home page has downloaded properly. Save visuals for the really important pages – for example, where you are displaying products
- consider copyright issues if you are using another's visuals or text from a different source
- if you have an online store, include an explanation of how to buy online and a reminder that there is a secure server (see 'Web security', opposite), to encourage potential customers to shop with you. Any order form should be simple
- a problem of many web sites is that they list items which are not in stock. A good e-shop will give an idea of delivery time
- give careful thought to including key words to describe parts of your site and guide users around it. Some search engines which users contact to look for themes or specific pages access some sites by picking out key words.

Once you have created your site, you need to get it published. It is essential to be well positioned on the Internet. Setting up a web site is rather like choosing a company name so that it will be easily found in the telephone directory. There are millions and millions of web sites. You have to ensure that your site is easily accessible – where your site sits in the listings of search engines is important (those high up in alphabetical order will appear first). A survey conducted by MORI in 2000 revealed that 75 per cent of Internet users were frustrated when searching for information on the Internet, and among those people 30 per cent said that they frequently did not find what they were looking for.

The first step is to acquire a proper domain name or Internet address, for example *www.yourcompanyname.co.uk*. Then you need to get the file transfer protocol server address (the entry code, if you like) from your service provider (the company you pay to connect you to the Web).

You have to visit the search engines (the reference libraries of the Internet that find web sites for users) you have chosen and enter your site. At the foot of their home pages they have a section called 'Add URL'. This leads to a page where you can enter your web site's details. Some search engines just want basic details, others want keywords and a description of your activities. Be warned: it can take three months or more to get those details taken up by the search engines, because they have thousands of new web sites added every day. So allow a long lead-in time before you get any response from your site. The main search engines in the UK are Excite, Altavista, Infoseek, Lycos, Yahoo!, Google UK and Jeeves UK.

Web security

If you are selling goods over the Internet, you will want to reassure those who visit your site that transactions are safe.

A secure link is indicated by a key or closed padlock on the browser toolbar or the letter 's' for secure in the Internet address after the 'http' prefix. Customers will also look for a logo that indicates that the trader complies with a code of good practice, such as the Which? Web Trader logo or the TrustUK e-hallmark (see below).

The Which? Web Trader logo and TrustUK e-hallmark

Which? Web Traders agree to meet and abide by a code of practice which ensures safe and convenient online shopping for consumers. When a company applies to Which? for permission to display the logo, Which? carries out tests to ensure that it is genuine and meets the standard requirements. Granting the logo does not imply that Which? recommends the actual goods or services offered or the customer service provided by the trader outside the areas covered by the code. After acceptance by the scheme, Which? carries out random checks to make sure the company is sticking to the code, and will investigate any reports that traders are not following the code. Full details of the scheme are at *www.which.net*

TrustUK is a government-backed scheme set up by the Alliance for Electronic Business and Consumers' Association. It ensures minimum standards for online codes of practice, including:

- a formal complaints procedure
- an efficient system for dispute resolution
- procedures to guarantee consumer privacy
- good practices to ensure the security of information people give over the Internet.

Maintaining your web site

The amount of energy and involvement devoted to e-commerce does not stop with setting up a web site. Once you have established a presence on the Internet, you need to set up links to specialist web sites that will be constantly read by your target market. Remember the model-train manufacturer on page 76? His web site ought to be linked to a model-train enthusiasts' online magazine. In addition you need to update the information on your site regularly, or appoint someone to do it for you. You should aim to review your web site at least once a quarter.

Business Internet packages

Although web sites can be a useful shop window, you should not feel compelled to set one up if your company does not really need one yet. If, however, you have a reason for needing a web site – perhaps because you want to sell internationally and your products are easy to ship, or you have employees who can provide a service anywhere in the world – investment in a business package which will do all the work for you and have you up and running in a few weeks is well worth it. This is known as 'web hosting'.

For example, for a small monthly fee British Telecom's service currently includes:

- a domain name (e.g. *www.yourcompanyname.co.uk*) and up to 20 email addresses
- credit-checking facilities and access to financial, business and travel information
- 20MB of web space
- d-i-y web-building tools
- access to a 24-hour helpdesk
- optional local area network (LAN) access for the whole business with up to 100 email addresses (£80 a month at the time of writing).

At the time of writing, BT Web Design is able to design and maintain a web site for businesses incorporating animated graphics, photographic images and order forms for a one-off fee of £150. The more expensive BT Web Publisher offers an advanced toolbox which aims to maximise customer experience and enables a more interactive web site. It also:

- collects customer information to improve a business's marketing
- allows customers to search for information on the site easily and quickly, saving them time and encouraging return visits
- enhances customer loyalty by giving customers access to exclusive areas via personal user names and passwords
- ensures that credit-card details are held safely and confidential data is transferred with secure file encryption.

These start-up packages are outlined in a *Guide to E-business Solutions*, available from British Telecom's e-business Advice Line.★ Plenty of other companies, such as Virginbiz.net,★ offer similar packages. At the time of writing, Virginbiz.net's *Get Going on the Internet* offers a free 45-day web site trial. This includes:

- a domain name (worth up to £100)
- an instant professional web card (a single-page starter web site) to promote your services online
- access to Virginbiz.net SiteBuilder tools to develop the web card into a multi-page web site
- expert technical and customer support
- up to 50 email addresses for employees
- unlimited access to the Internet.

Virginbiz.net also promotes company web sites by permitting a single submission of the company web site to major search engines; setting up a mini advertising campaign with 500 banner advertisements on the Net; supplying personalised Net cards for mailing to existing and potential customers; and letting the company register with Biznet's online trade directory.

Virginbiz.net publishes a *Quick Guide* showing how to build a multi-page web site quickly and easily, as well as a manual containing professional tips and *Profiting from the Internet*, a guide showing how businesses can benefit from being on the Web.

The Which? Online/ISP service offers unlimited Internet access, five email addresses and personal web space. Contact Which? Online★ for details.

M-commerce

M-commerce (the facility for carrying out e-business while on the move) is on the up, and has given the Internet a new lease of life. Figures released by Genie, the mobile Internet arm of British Telecom, showed that in the last quarter of 2000, WAP phone usage rose by an impressive 51.3 per cent.

At the moment, m-commerce is primarily a service for providing and exchanging information. E-tailers hope that WAP technology will give buying on the Internet a new lease of life.

WAP

Most people use WAP phones for online banking and travel information, to keep in contact with the office or check on orders while with a client. According to experts, by 2003 all mobile phones on sale will be WAP-enabled, and by 2005 the population will conduct business worth over £13 billion using WAP. Although the system currently has limitations, more than 200 mobile phone manufacturers, phone companies, Internet companies and software manufacturers have already signed up for WAP. The WAP specification can be downloaded from the Internet for free, so any business can start down the road of m-business.

Other systems

Other phone technology in addition to WAP includes GPRS (general packet radio system), also called '2.5 generation mobile protocol', which is a better and faster mobile phone. Likely to appear in 2004 is UMTS (universal mobile telephony system). The specifications of this third-generation mobile technology were agreed all over the developed world in 1999, which means that UMTS will be able to be used globally. The phones will have connection speeds of up to 2Mb, which will mean fast connections, fast data rates and multi-tasking among other attributes. The mobile phone company Orange has confirmed that it will be offering the following services: high-speed Internet access; e-commerce services such as home shopping and online booking; location-based information and entertainment services; mobile video-conferencing; and the ability to download movie clips, soundtracks and sports highlights.

Meanwhile a spokesman for the One2One mobile phone company recommends that businesses move applications to intranet and Web-based technology since this will provide 'maximum flexibility to deploy email, information and applications'. The spokesman advises talking to your accounts, email and Web suppliers to ensure you are geared up to use the Web for each aspect of your business.

M-commerce security

Secure and simple electronic payment methods need to be developed before m-commerce can really take off. Various options are being explored, such as the smart card, which carries all the necessary encrypted information for billing. This can be transmitted with one swipe of the card rather than having to enter all the transaction details, which is time-consuming and can be a security risk. It is likely that the card principle will evolve into a personalised microchip embedded in the phone, since the industry seems to want mobile phones to get smaller, not larger.

Another possibility is the digital signature, which would appear to be taken seriously as a contender since the EU has recently drafted a directive about it. A digital signature is similar to a PIN number used when trading on the Internet, but it requires e-tailers to have the relevant software and card reader so that they can decipher the information in the digital signature. An additional development is a 'universal shopping cart', which is rather like a high-street loyalty card. The m-shopper joins the scheme and is given an electronic password which allows him or her to shop with all the retailers who have signed up to the scheme, adding items to the shopping cart on the way and, with a single click at the checkout, paying for everything together.

The drawbacks of technology

In spite of the opportunities, no one really trusts technology. Even computer experts have problems designing foolproof fail-safe systems. The Which? Online survey described on page 75 showed that 51 per cent of Internet users have not yet purchased anything online and only 23 per cent of users think it is safe to use credit cards online – with some justification. The debate about computer security centres on public key infrastructure (PKI) technology, which is the convention and standard for most emerging technology.

E-errors

Examples abound of technology being subject to pitfalls. In August 2000, the energy company Powergen was forced to compensate thousands of customers after a customer logged on to its web site to pay his bill and discovered he was reading the unencrypted credit-card details, home addresses and payment records of himself and 7,000 other customers. Woolworth also had to shut down its online store in 2000 after customers' credit-card details and personal details were read by another user. In February 2000 the online directory Yahoo!, news service CNN and online bookshop Amazon were out of action for hours after hackers deliberately flooded them with junk emails in a 'denial of service attack'. A hacker also accessed the customer files of Safeway, sending an extremely damaging email to every one of them. The Halifax Building Society had to delay the opening of its online bank, Intelligent Finance, because of concerns about the security of the system. No wonder, since early in 2000 the online bank Egg had been the target of a serious attempted fraud which, according to industry experts, required very little technical skill.

Protecting your business

How many of us have stood inside a bank or building society that is unable to function *in any way* – cannot even take money from you – because the computer which controls everything, including the opening of the tills, has crashed? Reliance on technology makes your company very vulnerable unless you are punctilious about maintenance and, above all, taking backups and keeping them off-site in a secure place. So you need to be as careful about IT security as you do about the security of your business premises and stock.

It is almost impossible to stop cybercrime. A survey conducted in the UK in 2000 showed that more than half of the top 1,000 businesses had lost money through Internet abuse. With the introduction of computerised banking systems, businesses run the gamut of electronic error including overcharging (see Chapter 7). The deliberate transmission of viruses, fraud and electronic data theft are becoming commonplace. To counter this, make sure that you have a proper firewall – these can be downloaded from the Internet – and insure against electronic fraud with one of the specialist insurance firms that have set up for this sector of the market (see Chapter 13).

A waste of valuable time?

Beware of letting the Internet become a burden. Many people now receive 50 or 100 emails a day, and just finding the time to reply calls for good time management skills.

A survey done by Gallup and the Institute for the Future, a Californian thinktank, found that nearly half the emails received during the working day were unnecessary inter-departmental notes or nothing but gossip, chatter and jokes. Responding to emails, if not controlled, can depress the output of work that has real value. Regulations are now in place that give employers the power to monitor employees' communications, and many companies have drawn up codes of practice on email use to restrict abuse (see page 179).

The Gallup report mentioned above concluded that companies need to use technology more efficiently. The report also examined the use of mobile phones and suggested that they also generated a large percentage of unnecessary calls because they were so easy to use. Mobile phones also mean that many executives are constantly on call and can never relax. For advice on how to take time out from the demands of the 24-hour society, see Chapter 14.

The advantages of technology

Despite the problems associated with e-commerce and new technology, for most businesses the advantages outweigh the drawbacks. This section outlines just a few of them. The most significant innovations which are useful to SMEs are referred to throughout this book.

- Having the latest technology may mean that you can do without having a central office or at least minimise your overheads. Staff in service industries can work from home, keeping in touch by email (see Chapter 11 for more on flexible working). Drivers can stay in touch with headquarters using WAP phones (see above). Documents, photographs and diagrams can all be sent via email to whoever needs them. There is very little need to come into a central workplace at all. This could give your company an advantage if you are operating in a marketplace where responses need to be speedy and costs kept to a minimum. A city-centre office is an expense most companies would gladly do without.
- Even if you are not setting up a web site or expanding your market through the Internet as described on pages 89–92, the Web can be a useful source of information. Market reports and surveys are often published on the Internet.
- The Internet and new technology are traditionally the preserve of whizz-kids. This is an area where the old can learn from the young to the benefit of the business – see 'e-possums', page 45.
- Online, mobile and computerised banking can make life easier for SMEs (for information about these services, see pages 107–110).

E-commerce and the latest technology may feature in your company's growth or they may not. That depends upon your company's particular needs and the direction in which you choose to move. You can choose to ignore the people who are telling you that technology is the answer to everything. It may be the answer to some things. It could prove to be the route to success for your company. However, you have to be sure that there is a solid infrastructure and that your company has a sound basis for growth. The other chapters in this book will help you to establish that the building blocks are in place before you invest in technology.

Chapter 6

Developing your marketing strategy

The business is doing well. You have developed your products or services and built up a healthy bank of customers. Your accounts are in order and you have staff that you thoroughly trust and who are very productive. What could go wrong?

Unforeseen disasters aside, you could just be enjoying the glow of success a little too much to notice that the marketplace for your goods or services is changing. You may, for example, make luxury goods for the home and fail to react to a slump in the housing market, which might mean that people are not spending as much on the interior of their homes. You may become aware of that fact only when more and more retail outlets report that interior décor products are proving difficult to sell.

All types of business need to be aware of economic changes. Who could have foreseen, for example, that by the early 21st century three out of every five children aged between ten and twelve would have mobile phones? The mobile phone manufacturers had already recognised that the adult market was becoming saturated and so they began a marketing campaign to target children beginning secondary school. Previous campaigns had been successfully targeted at teenagers and women.

Obviously, the first symptom of a declining market is declining sales or orders that start to diminish in size. The trick is to get in before that happens and anticipate the market trends. This is what separates the top companies from those that just react to events.

Expanding your market through e-commerce

At the time of writing many small companies are probably panicking about the media hype about e-commerce (explained in

Chapter 5). The pressure to have a web site and the advertisements asking 'Are you ready?' are sending many thriving businesses into a spiral of self-doubt, even though the number of companies reaping rewards from trading on the Net is small. A 2001 survey carried out by the CBI and KPMG Consulting showed that more than three-quarters of businesses derived less than 5 per cent of sales from e-commerce, with traditional companies experiencing the least impact.

This pressure to enter the world of high-tech sales is also diverting many businesses from the real marketing challenges that they should be facing. It is important to focus on your existing markets before branching into e-commerce (see page 92). Look at the facts. The Internet, at the moment, is extremely useful if you are selling certain products, like books, that can be easily and inexpensively despatched nationally or internationally, or you are advertising high-priced services to a business market. It is not so good for:

- products which the customer really needs to see and feel (such as clothes or craft items)
- items which cannot be despatched easily or cheaply (because they are fragile or bulky)
- products which the customer traditionally expects to have on a free trial basis before buying
- products the customer can return by walking into a store.

The latest statistics on Internet use give some cause for concern (see page 78). But e-tailing on the Internet is not all doom and gloom. Interestingly, it is shaping up to follow just the same old principles as face-to-face marketing. Those companies that are predicted to do well on the Internet are high-street names such as Boots, Argos and Dixons. Why? Because, according to Verdict, the consumers know and trust the familiar names and they have somewhere to return the faulty goods. Just as Internet book publishers are finding that they cannot overcome the consumer's need to hold a proper book, other e-tailers are finding out that the British like to know there is a place they can go to if the product is unsatisfactory.

The outdoor equipment retailer

Sometimes a company can be successful by marrying the great strength of the Internet – access to information – with the business of e-tailing.

In autumn 1999, two young men set up a web site selling approximately 50 items of equipment for mountain biking, walking, hiking and climbing. The site was set up in response to the high-street outdoor equipment shops which, many outdoor enthusiasts felt, did not train their staff sufficiently and were often unable to give expert advice about the goods they sold. The new web site offered high-quality products but also lots of independent reviews and guides and a wealth of other information to help its potential customers, and visitors to the site could use it just as an information source if they wished. One of the greatest draws was a trip planner providing weather and traffic information, train timetables and hiking and biking route maps.

The company, very sensibly, kept it as a UK-only site for quite a while, as that was where their greatest market knowledge lay, but it has since expanded into Europe in a modest way as well as increasing its product range and information provision to cover snow and watersports.

There is no doubt that if you plan and manage it carefully, having a web site can greatly profit your business. For advice on this, see page 79. The Virginbiz.net★ guide *Profiting from the Internet* outlines the benefits of using the Internet as a marketing tool:

- using the Net as a shop window to attract customers
- helping customers find your company
- keeping valued customers online
- increasing your company's profile and credibility
- cutting the cost of marketing, publicity, customer contact and support and technical services.

Chapter 5 looks in more detail at the advantages and disadvantages of selling online, the phenomenon of the Internet and attitudes towards e-commerce.

Although e-tailing should not be seen as a shortcut to a fortune, you should nevertheless keep an eye on developments.

Home shopping via TV is a growth area. Shopping channels such as QVC emerged following the introduction of analogue satellite TV, and interactive shopping is now on offer from cable and digital TV companies. Customers can access a menu of options and choose goods according to type (electrical, toys, food, etc.) and retailer – typically high-street names. Some providers such as ONdigital offer Internet access instead, supplying a modem to allow the viewer to watch TV and surf the Net at the same time. By the end of 2001, ONdigital and similar companies expect to have made significant inroads into the home television Internet market.

Many shopping malls have hosted aggressive marketing campaigns by companies trying to sell TV Internet systems to the public. It may be that by 2002 the number of households with such systems may constitute a significant enough market sector for you to consider e-tailing. This would depend on whether you sell low volumes of high-priced goods or high volumes of low-priced goods.

Watching your existing markets

It is unlikely that you are selling to just one market segment. If you are, you may need to consider some diversification of your goods and services because relying on only one market segment is risky. If that segment should collapse through saturation, a change in economic circumstances or in fashions, then you would have no other target market to turn to and quickly enlarge upon.

For example, let us say that a travel company which makes a good profit out of coach holidays for senior citizens were suddenly to find that its customers were reluctant to take a coach tour again after a few high-profile coach crashes hit the headlines. If that travel company did not have other options that it could build up, such as activity hotel breaks aimed at the lower-income senior citizen, then it would go to the wall because it would not have diversified enough to be able to weather a change in the marketplace.

What you need is a market development strategy. Let us assume that you have a small company which manufactures soft hats – baseball caps, sun hats, babies' hats, and so on – and you employ ten women to sew these hats, as well as a handful of administrative staff.

Until now, all your contracts have been dictated by the clients. They design the hats and put the contracts out to tender, some of which you have been fortunate enough to secure. Until now you have specialised only in manufacturing, with no creative element at all, which has put you in the risky position of having to rely on the client companies for work. Have you thought about creating more work by being creative yourself – say, by employing someone who could design new hats and generate more business for you because you could now offer your clients a complete creative and manufacturing process, offering the designs and tying the manufacturing contract in with the design?

The home maintenance service company

In wealthier areas of the country, householders who are going to be away from their property for any length of time sometimes engage the services of local estate agents that offer a property-minding service. In the case of one such operation, the service had become lacklustre, to say the least, attracting complaints of indifference and lack of attention to detail. Owners frequently found that their properties were not cleaned in time for their return or the companies failed to make regular internal inspections to ensure that all was well.

An enterprising businesswoman, herself on the receiving end of this indifferent service, decided to set up a company which would offer a home maintenance service that would be of the highest quality and guaranteed performance. Her approach was a little different. She contacted all the property owners and cited the catalogue of complaints they had about their existing services. Then she offered them a superior service in return for a monthly fee (payable all year, whether the owners were in residence or not). The clients accepted this eagerly because what was also offered was a penalty clause. They would be able to reclaim their monthly fees if the maintenance company defaulted in any way. Thus the new company was able to take an existing market away from several other companies which had neglected to look after them.

The same approach could be applied to a service company – such as one that provides plants, horticultural displays and the maintenance service for offices, hotels and other public buildings. Perhaps your problem is that the local market is already saturated but you can only service an area within a 50-mile radius, otherwise operating costs begin to rise too much. Look at your core business. You have lots of plants and you employ people who know how to present those plants to advantage and how to look after them. All your employees also have spacious transport in order to carry these plants around. How can you develop a new marketplace without expanding too much and having to find more finance? Think of new markets for what you do. How about floral decorations for parties? Or what about targeting the large houses in your area whose occupants have no time but lots of money and would welcome a plant maintenance system, either indoors or outdoors?

Keeping up with social and business trends

Keeping ahead of the marketplace means being in touch with what is going on around you. To a certain degree it means networking – time-consuming though that may be. It also means taking the latest trade journals, going to trade exhibitions, meeting other business people for lunch, reading widely and watching as much of life around you as you can.

If you are manufacturing or providing a service for, say, the lucrative children's market you need to have your finger on the pulse of what is going to be 'big' next year. Perhaps that suggests you should visit America or Japan to find out what trends are going to come into the UK in the next six months. It is possible that you could get government assistance to fund an overseas trip – contact the DTI★ to see what schemes are on offer to help exporters, or your local Chamber of Commerce (via the British Chambers of Commerce★) to find out if it organises any cheap travel deals.

Keeping your eyes and ears open is important since nothing changes as fast as today's markets and consumer goods. A good example of how quickly markets can alter is the way in which media attention on GM foods suddenly whipped up the demand for organic produce in supermarkets. Before the year 2000, the organic food sections of supermarket shelves had represented a very low proportion of the foods on offer. In the space of one year, public demand caused the supermarkets to expand their organic ranges almost overnight. Now, some of the chains claim to stock in the region of 1,000 to 2,000 organic products.

When more means less

Finding new markets can sometimes mean narrowing your range of products or services, rather than expanding it. The marketplace you started selling in may be saturated or fading, and finding a new one may mean that you have to specialise rather than diversify. Many business consultancies, in the last few years, have found that being general management consultants is not especially lucrative in a world where such services are two-a-penny. For many, becoming more specialised – as energy consultants, tax consultants, human resources consultants and so on – generates far more business.

This approach applies to other fields. For example, a group practice of complementary medicine therapists could find that the local area has become saturated with similar services and, by deciding within the group to specialise in the health problems of children, or sportsmen and -women, say, they could carve out a new market which they will have to themselves for a while.

Sometimes, 'going upmarket' can be the very thing to give a product a new lease of life. This might mean making it more luxurious so that it appeals to people who appreciate quality, snobs or nostalgics. For example, a clock case made of rosewood with inlays, instead of cheap metal, will appeal to a particular sector of the market. Transforming the services of a hairdressing salon into a 'head-to-toe' beauty experience, with a diet lunch thrown in, could attract the customers who like to be pampered occasionally rather than having a basic cut-and-blow-dry.

To specialise rather than diversify requires a very accurate reading of current trends and a good perception of needs. You need to define your market.

Defining your market

Many businesses start off finding a market niche which they have a hunch exists and are able to exploit. Once a business is up and running, depending on hunches which are unsupported by evidence can be the factor that brings the business to an abrupt end before it reaches its third or fourth birthday. Now is the time to do those marketing exercises you should have done at the outset but perhaps did not have time for (see box).

Consolidating a position of strength

Before expanding your marketing strategies, you need to apply similar criteria to your existing market. It is certainly a bad idea to

---

Defining the market: a checklist

1 What market is it that you want to enter?
2 Why is that market different from other markets?
3 How many markets are similar but not quite the same?
4 Will any of those similar markets take business away from you?
5 What is the size of your chosen market? (Is it international, national, regional, local? Can you find out numbers of potential customers?)
6 How would you contact that market? (Advertisements, mail-shots, email, web site, etc.)
7 What are the preferred distribution channels of that market? (Do you know if your target audience would prefer to buy your product from a mailshot, in a shop, through a magazine, through an agent? If you offer a service would people prefer to use it because of recommendations, seeing you at a trade fair, through a trade magazine etc.?)
8 What are the threats to your intended market? (Change in tastes, another company launching a better product, a change in the economic climate when you are trying to sell a luxury item, etc.?)
9 Does your product/service have a limited lifespan, which is bound to be reflected in the longevity of its market? (You may be an energy consultant who does energy audits and shows companies how to save money on their energy bills. Once you have done that for them, they have no further need of your services. Or you may manufacture a product which is guaranteed to last for ten years, which will inevitably mean that the market reaches a saturation point.)

---

abandon a product or service which, until now, has been a reason-able source of revenue. You may be able to boost your position even if sales have stagnated or are dropping off. Ask yourself the follow-ing question: what more can you do to revive a flagging market? Note the word 'flagging', not 'disappearing'. There is precious little you can do if a market is disappearing because it is saturated, or your product has been replaced by a more relevant one, or your services

10 Has any other company attempted to enter your intended mar-ket and, if so, how did it fare? If you read the relevant trade magazines and the business sections of national newspapers, you may have read about such attempts. It may be a subject of gossip at the local Chamber of Commerce, or the company that succeeded in its attempt may have actually issued a press release. Gathering market intelligence like this is very much, again, about networking.

11 If you are facing competition in your intended marketplace, how does the opposition position itself? (In other words, what methods of selling and distributing or functioning does the opposition favour? Is there any competitive advantage in your choosing another method?)

12 What will give you an edge in your intended market? (For example, can you provide a similar product that is cheaper, or a service that is faster?)

13 If you have a long-term strategy, do you know whether the intended market will be ongoing? (Think about children's products or services. They tend to be age-banded. Do you know if you are about to hit a baby boom or a big slump in the number of toddlers within your target market over the next few years? You need to know the figures. Similarly with the elderly: you need statistics. You may manufacture or import a sub-stance that alleviates a particular ailment but Department of Health figures may show that this disorder is becoming less common. You have to know the long-term prospects if you want a long-term strategy.)

are no longer sought because everyone is making cutbacks. If you think your hitherto profitable market is flagging, you may find it helpful to work your way through the checklist in the box below.

Finding new markets abroad

Probably the most risky way of expanding a market, selling abroad requires a great deal of groundwork. National differences can be significant and regulations are frequently dissimilar to those in the UK. Many companies have fallen foul of other countries' advertising regulations, which, in the main, are far less relaxed than in the UK or the USA.

Cultural differences

It is extraordinary how the British and the Americans cherish their own cultural value-systems and are quite astonished when products

---

Consolidating the market: a checklist

1 Can you devote more time to selling your company? If your area of operation is business-to-business then perhaps you just need to raise your profile a bit more.

2 Can you tread water until the trends change again or your target age group (remember those children) rises? Are you convinced, or has past experience taught you, that your product/s will come back into fashion again – like the yo-yo and skateboards?

3 Can you create a new fashion? For example, at a price, you can bid to have your product 'placed' in a popular children's television series or a major children's film. This has proved to be a good method of creating a 'fashion' for an item. But, obviously, these trends change so fast that it would really only give you some breathing space to diversify or find a new market (perhaps overseas).

4 Can you lower prices without causing financial difficulties within your company? This may be one way of dealing with a market that is flagging due to too much competition.

5 Can you repackage? Many confectionery manufacturers have managed to keep certain brands popular for many years by periodically giving them a new image.

---

or services are rejected or do not do as well as they did in their home country. When Spain joined the EC there was a stampede to Madrid of UK marketing directors hoping to get a foothold in the lucrative Spanish market which had been closed when General Franco was alive. When they discovered that the Spanish had quite different interests, prejudices and taboos from the British, astonishment and confusion were rife. Some products failed miserably and some were successful apparently against the odds. One biscuit manufacturer in the Midlands discovered to his delight that the Spanish adored all the plain biscuits that the British found rather boring and he had been on the point of discontinuing.

All kinds of surprises may be in store when you seek foreign customers. To quote some findings on national preferences revealed in recent years:

6 Can you market your business in a different way? Perhaps the way in which you sell is not reaching enough of your target market. Look at your options. If you place advertisements in magazines, consider whether direct mail shots could achieve a better response. If you are in the business-to-business sphere, would mass fax transmissions help you reach the right people more effectively than a mail shot? There are plenty of options – perhaps a marketing consultancy could help.

7 Can you get out there and network a bit more? Form alliances, forge friendships – out of such things come business opportunities. Other people's ideas, casually mentioned over lunch, can be the spark that ignites a flame. Casual conversations at trade fairs and exhibitions can generate ideas that could open up new markets.

8 Do your employees have any ideas? (Always ask – you can get some real nuggets of wisdom from this source.) Good managers realise that, often, production staff or other employees are far more involved with the end-users of a company's products or services than management and they can frequently come up with simple solutions to problems because their view is uncluttered by other considerations.

- the typical Frenchman uses almost twice as many cosmetics and beauty aids as does his wife
- the Germans and French eat more packaged, branded spaghetti than do the Italians
- Italian children like to eat a bar of chocolate between two slices of bread as a snack
- the Basques adore custard cream biscuits
- the Czechs prefer to buy canned vegetables rather than fresh
- the Chinese generally do not eat dairy products.

Useful organisations and sources of help

Finding new markets abroad requires help. Fortunately there are many organisations to which one can turn. The Institute of Export* exists to raise the standards of export management and practice through education and training and produces a great deal of useful information. The DTI* has an export section which deals specifically with overseas market information. It is always able to advise on the potential market for British business, whatever the field. Its recommendations are based on feedback from the commercial sections of the British embassies worldwide. The detailed information may include statistics, breakdowns of market segments and sizes and an outline of possible market gaps as well as advice on laws, regulations, currency problems and political situations. It can sometimes help with the funding of overseas trips and other matters.

The Export Clubs* movement comprises over 70 nationwide clubs. Some are very well known in their respective geographical areas while others are less so; all of them strive to enable British businesses to become more successful at selling into overseas markets. The clubs are run by local business people and approximately half have close connections with Chambers of Commerce, while in some areas links are in place with the Institute of Export. Representatives from the DTI regional offices regularly attend Export Clubs meetings, frequently as speakers. The key objective is to stimulate interest and activity in export trade and the clubs provide a useful forum where the inexperienced can meet and discuss selling overseas with experienced exporters. Another source of information and guidance is the British Exporters Association (BExA),* which represents all kinds of British exporting companies but particularly export houses.

Service-providing companies might start by approaching their own trade associations, if they have one, to see if they have a department that advises on exporting. Many of the major accountancy firms are now global and have offices in most countries. Accountancy firms can also advise on the export potential of services in certain countries.

Companies thinking of expanding overseas might find translation software useful (see page 103).

Export houses

These are companies that handle the business of exporting for small to medium-sized companies which do not wish, or are not large enough, to have their own export department. Export houses can provide a full service for the would-be exporter, mainly handling all the minutiae of paperwork involved in exporting. The BExA publishes a list of members including export houses.

Export agents

Export agents are in a unique position to help UK manufacturers enter a new export market. They sell a manufacturer's goods in a selected country or countries about which they have expert knowledge, and negotiate transactions in either their own name or that of the manufacturer. Like all agents they operate mostly on a commission basis, although some negotiate flat fees for certain long-standing sales contracts. This can prove to be a cost-effective way of expanding into new markets and, for new exporters, business can be secured with minimal exposure.

There are also several categories of buying houses, merchants and foreign store-buyers who regularly visit the UK to buy goods on behalf of their employers or clients. The BExA produces the *Directory of Export Buyers in the UK*, which eases the task of finding the right representation. It lists all the categories of agents as well as the geographical areas and products in which they specialise.

Expanding your market through computer technology

Computer technology has enabled many businesses to expand into new and exciting markets with great ease. Consumers can now buy all kinds of goods and services through the information systems on their television (see page 92), via the Internet or by telephone (see

Chapter 5). Some companies hardly ever touch cash any more – all their sales are made by credit-card transaction. A well-known example is Amazon.com, the online retailer.

Investing in new technology can help you to achieve a marketing edge. Giving your salesforce laptop or notebook computers or WAP phones so that they can email or fax orders the moment they are placed can give your company the reputation for being fast and efficient (provided those orders are filled swiftly, of course). It may also mean that you will not need a central office, or can at least cut down on overheads.

Store and loyalty cards

Many large retailers, such as Debenhams, Allders and House of Fraser, introduced store cards because they were the most effective way of gathering market information about their customers' preferences and peak buying times. All this information was put to good use when planning their buying, stock control and sales drives. They were able to target customers with product information more effectively because they had the names and addresses of 'loyal' shoppers. More importantly, when some of the retailers decided to move into the business of selling financial services they had a ready-made mailing list.

Store cards have worked reasonably well because they are, in effect, a credit card which enables the shopper to shop in a particular store 'on account'. This has proved popular with women making impulse purchases or buying clothing.

Other companies, such as the major supermarkets, introduced loyalty cards which merely 'banked', through electronic transfer of the data on the loyalty card, a number of credits in the customer's 'account', to be redeemed either against their shopping bill or later for other goods, which could be at the store in question or at another retail outlet signed up to the scheme. However, some supermarkets have abandoned 'loyalty' cards because they have found that, in the fickle world of food retail, they do not work. Customers are more interested in going where the food is cheaper, or where they can park, than collecting loyalty points.

Buying marketing lists

Lists of customers' names and addresses are often held on databases. It is possible for smaller companies to purchase lists of target markets from professional market research organisations, which are constantly conducting surveys, or from list brokers which collate credit-card information or other data that they have purchased from large companies. The Market Research Society* should be able to provide information about list brokers.

Translation software

One piece of technology that could help considerably if you were contemplating expanding into overseas markets would be to install a translation software package. These offer the facility to translate English text into many different languages. Sending letters of enquiry to overseas companies could achieve nothing if they are not in a language that will be understood by the recipient. For a translation program to work successfully, the original text must be very precise, and grammatically correct. The software cannot come up with accurate translations of colloquialisms.

It is quite difficult to produce a good translation by computer. A service that offers a mixture of computer and human translation is now available via the Internet. Certain ISPs and major web sites offer free computer translation for simple documents such as letters, with an option for the user to pay a modest additional fee and have the document checked over by a human translator and emailed back. The advantage of using this is that you do not have to buy and install the translation software if you have only an occasional need for such a service. The US sites *www.freetranslation.com* and *http://babelfish.altavista.com* offer translation by computer.

The Internet

For tips on how the Internet can help your business, see 'Expanding your market through e-commerce' (page 89). Even if you are not planning to sell goods or services online, the Internet can be a useful source of information. If you read in the media that a survey or market report has been published which is of interest to you – on a particular segment of the population, say – the Internet is a good place to look for full details. Usually such reports are published online. You may get the whole report or just a taster, the rest of the information being available only on payment of a fee.

Chapter 7

Managing money

This chapter suggests ways in which your business can interact more efficiently with banks and the Inland Revenue.

Dealing with banks

The relationship with your bank should be a two-way exchange. New technology has introduced some convenient options for small businesses, such as computerised banking, but all too often banks are keener to take advantage of SMEs than to assist them, and many companies have been crippled by banks overcharging. In addition, banks often make errors when processing transactions which can be complicated to remedy. Unfortunately, owner/managers are often unwilling to complain because they are wary of jeopardising a key business relationship and lack the time to lodge a formal protest.

Some sole traders make the mistake of not separating out their personal finances from their business transactions. Even if you have a small operation, you should always differentiate between the two in order to run both strands more efficiently.

Banking problems and the need for regulation

In spring 2001 the Competition Commission declared that small businesses were being charged too much for loans and current accounts (see 'Overcharging problems', below). It also revealed that banking systems routinely make it difficult for SMEs trying to switch to another supplier (running two accounts with separate banks in parallel for a month or two may be the best way of easing the transition). These findings came as no surprise to the Federation of Small Businesses,* which also criticises banks for failing to provide sufficient information, such as a firm's credit history, to other banks. Without this, the firm could be seen as an unacceptable risk and other companies would be reluctant to accept it as a new customer. Businesses that are borrowing money are particularly vulnerable to key details not being passed on. The complexity of having to deal with the system prevents many businesses from switching, even though they are unhappy with their current service.

The government continues to monitor the financial services sector. In 2000, the Cruickshank Report concluded that banks need stronger regulation. The report, entitled *Competition in Banking*, published the findings of an independent government 1998 investigation into the banking industry which looked at whether banks meet the needs of groups including small businesses. In August 2000 the government stated that it encouraged the publication of comparative tables of banking products as well as tables showing complaints against financial services firms.

The Banking Code offers some measure of protection to personal (as opposed to business) customers by requiring that banks act fairly and responsibly. It states that banks should offer services and products that fit customer requirements and comply with regulations, consider cases of financial difficulty and arrears sympathetically and positively, ensure security and confidentiality, correct errors and handle complaints speedily. The Code is voluntary but a bank could be accused of breaking its provisions if a court of law deems that a contract was implied by the Code and that the bank has defaulted. The government is currently looking into the possibilty of developing a form of the Code that applies to SMEs.

The need for human contact
The growing trend towards online banking by banks and building societies means that it is becoming more and more difficult for people running a business to speak to a human being about their financial situation. Although most banks still have 'business advisers' or 'business managers' available, the chances are that you will have to go over the details of your account(s) with a different person from scratch every time. This can be inconvenient for developing businesses, which are often in need of one-to-one assistance and an informed, consistent approach. It might be worth investigating the business packages on offer from foreign banks based in the UK, which claim to offer customer-friendly service.

Overcharging problems

It is estimated that over £5 billion of overcharges is currently waiting to be reclaimed from banks. This situation has led to the emergence of a clutch of bank charge auditors – companies that investigate bank charges, overdrafts and loans on behalf of small and medium-sized businesses and negotiate with banks to resolve any errors or disputes that have arisen. Each of the high-street banks has an established negotiating team to handle the claims of bank charge auditors.

Only a handful of bank charge auditors exist in the UK, but these companies are extremely busy. Their customer base is diverse. For example, clients of Anglia Business Associates★ (ABA) Ltd, the UK's largest bank charge auditor and now owned by Consumers' Association, include corner shops, property developers, farmers, major league football clubs, bakers, builders, nursing homes and garages. Of these, Anglia's MD, Ian Foyster, estimates that at least 75 per cent have claimable refunds. In the course of their work, bank charge auditors have been able to claim refunds for customers ranging from a few thousand pounds to well over £100,000. Like good accountants, bank charge auditors can be recommended by your business colleagues and friends – but not, of course, by banks.

Ian Foyster offers this advice for account holders who are worried about overcharging:

- tabulate all the charges that you see in your bank statements
- look for any irregularities – e.g. a £5 charge that suddenly moves to £10 then to £15 over a relatively short period of time – say, within a year
- expect the banks to convince you that nothing is wrong
- stay alert and do not feel embarrassed about complaining
- request a copy of the bank's complaints procedure.

Most bank charge auditors charge a flat fee for the initial audit and then a percentage of the monies recovered for the negotiation and recovery service.

ABA regularly publishes, for the benefit of its customers, league tables that monitor banks' response times and reactions to customer complaints.

Overcharging refunds

- ABA negotiated an £87,000 refund from Lloyds TSB for a second-division football club in November 2000. The bank had failed to offset credit balances against borrowings, contrary to agreement.

- NatWest awarded a trout farmer in Norfolk a refund of £8,600. ABA found that he had been unfairly charged penal interest for payments that had been authorised.

- A Welsh building contractor received a £10,000 refund from its bank after ABA pointed out that unauthorised borrowing rates had been applied for a protracted period. The bank was found responsible for the error.

- A farmer in the Midlands received a £230,000 refund when ABA discovered significant overcharging on his current and loan accounts.

21st-century banking

Businesses now have the option of banking direct via a computer link or over the Internet, and other choices are opening up as new technology develops.

Computerised banking

Many banks have provided a computer link to their business customers ('direct connection') since the mid-1990s. This facility is most useful to larger companies. Typically a company can make payments to employees and suppliers, receive payments from customers and obtain balance and transaction information, among other services. The packages on offer require a computer, modem and special software from the bank. Customers' details are protected by security measures such as passwords.

At the moment, direct connections are more efficient than online banking at handling large volumes of transactions – for example, a large payroll. It is also possible to download account data to other software packages such as Microsoft Excel, Lotus 123 and Sage with direct connection banking, and immeasurably simpler to transfer money between overseas accounts and to exchange currencies. Note that things may not go smoothly if the direct connection does not interface easily with your business's software system – always check compatibility with your bank.

Direct connection services attract a large number of subscribers. NatWest and Barclays BusinessMaster each claim over 50,000 customers for their business services, while HSBC has over 30,000 clients for its Hexagon service.

Online banking

Online banking has been marketed as a system that will benefit both banks and their customers. To participate, you need an internet service provider (ISP). With this type of banking you can check balances and pending transactions, pay bills and transfer funds. Access to customer accounts is achieved by passing through security checks. A fast modem connection is desirable as it can take time to download information (cable or ADSL is best). An advantage of online over direct-link computerised banking is that it can be done from any computer with Internet access.

The Internet-based services offer similar functions to computerised banking, but it is well to remember that they are in the early stages of development. They do not, as yet, allow as much flexibility as the direct connection accounts, and so they are currently targeted at small to medium-sized businesses whose requirements are not as complex as those of larger organisations.

The Internet bank's blunder

A UK businesswoman opened a deposit account with an offshore-based Internet bank. The system wrongly opened not one, but three accounts in her name. When she posted the necessary documentation giving proof of identity to activate the account and start it earning interest, the bank activated one of the two accounts in her name that did not contain any money. Some time later, when querying why she had not received any interest, she discovered the bank's mistake. After 30 emails and countless telephone calls, the bank finally apologised and paid her £500 in compensation and £300 lost interest.

In spite of the limitations, research shows that the Internet banking services have captured the imagination of the business community. The greatest advantage to the busy owner/manager seems to be out-of-hours banking. Statistics from the Co-op Bank in 2000 show that the largest concentration of hits on its Internet banking site take place between 7a.m. and 9a.m. and between 6p.m. and 8p.m. The ability to make transactions out of office hours has proved to be the biggest draw. Online banks based in the USA have found that small businesses in particular value the ability to move money around various accounts, pay bills and check information without having to visit their bank to do so.

Online banking certainly seems to be attracting SMEs, albeit slowly. Current research indicates that it is used by 27 per cent of SMEs. Major banks that offer online services include Lloyds TSB (which reports that 200–500 firms a day are signing up), Barclays, NatWest and HSBC. There is also a variety of online banks which do not have a presence in any high street, such as Egg (which does not offer current accounts), Smile, Cahoot and First Direct, which have mainly targeted the personal banking market.

New developments

The banks constantly try to come up with add-ons that will put their online banking service ahead of those of their rivals. Features such as hourly updates of statements have been popular. For businesses, the new web sites set up by banks are the most interesting development. NatWest's site at *www.NatWestBusinessOnline.co.uk* allows users to conduct credit enquiries and also look through a database for new suppliers. Lloyds TSB's site at *www.success 4 business.com* is similar.

Some banks now offer interactive services via digital TV. This development, still in its infancy, enables you to transfer funds, check balances and operate multiple accounts. Flexibility varies from bank to bank, and compatibility of technology is obviously essential – for example, if your bank were to team up exclusively with, say, a digital cable company, you might not be able to use their service if you were a digital satellite subscriber. In addition, bank statements cannot be printed out until special printers for TVs become available. TV banking is aimed primarily at the individual consumer, but may be of interest to those time-strapped owner/managers mentioned earlier.

At the time of writing, HSBC and Abbey National have opened branches on the Open Channel (accessed through Sky Digital) and Barclays has a site on Cable Digital, while ONdigital offers Internet banking via its ONnet service. NatWest had yet to establish a site, although research carried out by the bank during the latter half of the 1990s found that people were quite interested in viewing statements and paying bills via television. However, research carried out by Barclays revealed that consumers were concerned that TV banking would compromise privacy.

Mobile banking is now possible using a WAP mobile phone. Currently mobile banking allows you to pay bills, transfer money and check balances, but the technology is in its infancy and WAP phones cannot display much information. Forthcoming phone systems promise faster services which will enable people to stay in touch with their finances on the move. For more information see page 84.

Security problems

It is clear that however you choose to conduct your bank transactions – via computer, television or mobile phone – the banks have yet to overcome security problems. In summer 2000 Barclays was forced to shut down its online banking services twice after customers complained that they were presented with other people's accounts.

Difficulties of this sort have resulted in the banks having to build security systems which require additional measures, such as the smart card. This technology is in its infancy, but will become more widespread in future. The smart card works rather like a credit card and requires a PC with a smart-card reader. Each person who needs to get into an online bank account is issued with an individual smart card, and the system has to read and validate this card before it will allow the user to gain access. Some banks are experimenting with digital certification, electronic IDs and passwords. In spite of these developments and the latest encryption software, the banks are still a long way from ensuring watertight technology. A computer expert at a major software manufacturer doubts whether 'there is really such a thing, or will ever be such a thing, as a totally secure computer system'.

In addition to these drawbacks, the most obvious disadvantage of online banking is that you still cannnot withdraw or pay in cash.

Complaining about banks and financial advisers

If you have experienced difficulties with a financial institution, you should make a formal complaint to the bank or building society first of all. If it fails to deal with your case in a satisfactory manner, you can contact regulatory organisations that will investigate your complaint. Banks are governed by the Banking Ombudsman Scheme (BOS),★ which received almost 13,000 complaints in 1999. Building societies are covered by the Buildings Societies Ombudsman (BSO),★ which received just over 1,000 complaints in 1999.

If you have problems with a financial adviser, raise the matter with the individual or the company employing him/her. If you do not obtain redress, contact the Financial Services Authority (FSA).★ Complaints about financial advisers continue to rise, and escalated from 9,000 in 1998 to 11,000 in 1999.

Always put any queries in writing and ask for a written reply, as having a record of communication between your company and the institution/adviser will help your case and be useful to lawyers.

Dealing with the Inland Revenue

This book is not the place to discuss the minutiae of tax matters. The Inland Revenue (IR)★ is the first stop if you need information on specific aspects of tax, and it has a user-friendly web site. Advice on tax regulations is also given in various Which? publications.★

A good accountant should be able to help you with tax matters. You could employ a part-time tax consultant to advise on the current regulations and deal with tax returns and administration. Some consultants are retired IR inspectors who have intricate knowledge of the system.

How growth may affect your tax status

Until now you may have had a relatively trouble-free relationship with the IR because you are a self-employed sole trader, which means that you and your business have the same identity. You may have been working from home, which gives you the benefit of being able to claim part of the running costs of your home against any income. However, two factors may put an end to that self-employed status.

First, you may need to expand to become a company and an employer, and to make yourself an employee of that company. Second, the IR might decide that you do not qualify as a self-employed person any more. This has happened to many contractors and consultants who were previously able to set up service companies or partnerships and hire out their own services to clients. This arrangement had tax and National Insurance advantages for the self-employed individuals. However, since April 2000 under the IR35 ruling such people are now classed as employees of the client company.

Once you develop into a limited liability company, you have to deal with a greater number of bureaucratic procedures. For example, you have to file accounts with Companies House★ or the Companies Registry★ in Northern Ireland on a regular basis, and your accounts must be audited. You may get a share of any company profits if you are a shareholder and/or an employee. Finance may be easier to raise, and you may find it easier to get trade credit. You will have bigger tax and National Insurance bills.

A partnership is another expansion route if you began as a sole trader. It is possibly easier to administer than a limited liability company because the IR regards partnerships as simply a collection of sole traders and therefore treats you as such for tax purposes. Although you have to fill out a tax return for the whole partnership, each individual partner is responsible for his or her individual tax arrangements. Any loss or profit the partnership makes is shared equally between the partners when it comes to assessment.

Business owners must deal with several employee-related taxes. Many employers have to administer schemes such as working families tax credit and disabled person's tax credit, while student loan repayments must be deducted from the payroll. Most accountants are tax experts and should be able to guide you through the basics.

The IR and e-business

The IR declares that it is seeking actively to encourage e-business in the UK and intends to offer a variety of electronic and online services to customers. At the time of writing, the IR already offers self-assessment filing over the Internet along with various electronic purchasing options.

The IR's e-business strategy was formulated in January 2001. It proposes to increase the number of electronic entry routes for customers and to introduce new forms of interaction (including conducting business through third parties). While trialling new approaches, the IR asserts that it will take on board customer feedback. Its stated aim is to 'close the digital divide' and to move away from being seen as a regulating body to an enabling one.

The IR's web site at *www.inlandrevenue.gov.uk/e-commerce/ sme4.htm* deals specifically with e-commerce issues. It covers topics such as tax relief, tax incentives for investment, trading on the Internet and the tax treatment of domain names.

IR powers on tax evasion

Changes in the law have given the IR stronger powers than ever to crack down on tax evasion. In 1999 the organisation was given the right to investigate companies without having to produce a reason. Previously, it was rather like the police – who cannot arrest someone without grounds for suspicion – in that it was unable to scrutinise a business unless it could justify its action.

In 2000 the IR acquired the right to immediate access to sensitive documents without having to obtain a search warrant to enter premises. In addition, from January 2001 magistrates' courts as well as the high courts were given the power to prosecute tax evasion. This will undoubtedly mean more prosecutions as more court time will be available.

Common tax errors

There are three reasons why people fall foul of the tax authorities:

- inexperience and poor record-keeping
- bad advice
- dishonesty.

Inexperience and poor record-keeping
Many proprietors of small and emerging companies fail to keep proper records and insist on doing all the book-keeping themselves instead of delegating the task to an accountant. Often, they make the mistake of concentrating on the business to so great an extent

that they fail to set up proper financial (including tax) management systems.

Many small companies regard the IR as 'the enemy' instead of going to the organisation for advice. In fact, since spring 2000 the IR has been actively trying to help small businesses by setting up telephone advice lines, hosting workshops and sending support teams out in the field. The IR should be your first port of call if you need help with tax matters.

Bad advice

The second reason for getting in trouble with the IR is through bad advice. There are plenty of 'creative' accountants who either do not tell their clients everything they should or try to persuade their clients to take advantage of this loophole and that dodge.

Although there are a huge number of regulations and different taxes, owner/managers should make an effort to keep up with the current legislation themselves, rather than relying on accountants to keep them informed. Contact the IR for help and advice.

Dishonesty

The third reason why people get into trouble with the tax authorities is the most obvious one – not being honest. The IR's investigative powers were topped up by the government because a great deal of small-scale fraud exists (see 'IR powers on tax evasion', above). Needless to say, it is not advisable to jeopardise your business for the sake of doing the tax man out of a few thousand pounds. SMEs are better advised to spend money on getting the best possible tax advice which, in the long run, could save them far more money than any fraud, which tax inspectors will inevitably discover. Prosecution for fraud can mean ruin. The current punishment is up to seven years in jail and/or an unlimited fine.

Penalties for late submission of tax forms

At the end of January 2001 just under a million people failed to file their completed self-assessment tax forms by the appointed deadline. They were automatically fined £100 plus annual interest of 8.5 per cent on the tax outstanding, to be charged at a daily rate until the bill was settled. Those who had not paid by the end of February 2001 were liable for a further surcharge of 5 per cent, with persistent offenders facing another £100 fine and 5 per cent surcharge in July 2001. After this point miscreants would face prosecution for non-payment of tax which, as stated earlier, can now be done in the magistrates' court. At the time of writing the penalties are a £500 fine and/or a six-month prison sentence.

Help with your tax return

Rather than getting into the position described above, ensure that you have the requisite expertise in place to get help quickly. The accountant/consultant route is one way. There are now companies in most major towns that specialise in filling in self-assessment tax forms – NatWest owns a chain called Tax Direct, and specialists include Tax Guard, Tax Team and Tax Assist. Your local telephone directory should produce some options (look under 'Tax experts').

Most high-street banks offer a tax advice and form-filling service for individuals, which could be useful for the self-employed or one-man/woman businesses. Most of the banks and the tax form services mentioned above charge between £50 and £300 depending upon how complicated the tax return is and where your business and/or tax adviser are located.

The Which? TaxService★ will collate your personal and financial details and fill out the correct information on your tax return form. Currently the fee is £49.99 for Which? members or £99.99 for non-members. You simply have to fill in a questionnaire, then, when the service has filled out the tax form you check it, sign it and send it back.

The IR offers to do the calculations for you. However, you have to start the process very early and send the paperwork in by September, as opposed to sending in your own assessment and tax due by January of the next year. You should also check the figures carefully.

Technology

Many tax software packages are available. Once you have loaded one of these into your computer and keyed in the details of your earnings, expenses, pensions, benefits, investments and bank statements and so on it will automatically calculate your tax liability and prepare a summary.

The IR accepts payment by a range of methods but is encouraging taxpayers to pay electronically by Internet or telephone banking. For more information, see the IR web site *www.ir-efile.gov.uk*. In January 2001, over 30,000 people filed their tax returns in this way.

TaxCalc 2001

The TaxCalc products from Which? Software* are the UK's best-selling self-assessment taxation programs.

- **TaxCalc Lite** is free (downloadable from *www.taxcalc.com*). It covers the core return, employment, self-employment and share schemes and allows you to file your return by Internet where it is enabled by the Inland Revenue.
- **TaxCalc 2001** costs £24.99. It covers the individual return and all supplementary pages except for Lloyd's Names, MPs (including SMPs and MWAs) and seafarers and calculates capital gains including indexation and taper relief (but not share pooling). It also covers family tax credits, children's tax credits and the R40 repayment claim return, and allows filing by Internet where it is enabled by the Inland Revenue. Most small business users are covered by TaxCalc as it includes the self-employment pages and, for those trading via a limited company, the employment pages.
- **TaxCalc for Small Partnerships** costs £44.99. It includes the short partnership return (i.e. all partnerships other than those which have untaxed investment income or partnership capital gains) and enables the preparation of individual returns for all partners. It also includes the R40 repayment claim return.
- **TaxCalc Plus** costs £129. This is the version for professional users, accountants, financial advisers and solicitors. It includes a licence allowing for an unlimited number of clients; the individual return and all supplementary pages except for Lloyd's Names, MPs (including SMPs and MWAs) and seafarers; both the short and full partnership returns; the R40 repayment claim return; and the ability to monitor the progress of all clients' returns.

The web site of the UK Taxation Directory at *www. uktax.demon.co.uk* lists contact details for a vast array of support services and technology that can assist you with tax matters. This is an independently compiled catalogue of web sites of potential interest to tax professionals and others seeking online information on UK tax matters. It is a very well constructed web site full of links to other sites, and can help you make an informed choice about where to go for assistance. With a click of your mouse you can be connected to:

- government sources
- professional bodies
- the tax profession (e.g. accountants and lawyers who specialise in tax matters)
- publishers of tax books
- publishers of tax software
- taxation recruitment specialists
- conferences, education and training.

The Taxation Directory also offers an email directory of tax professionals, a section on international taxes and a UK taxation bookstore in association with Amazon.co.uk.

Administering finances

Web-based services can help businesses to streamline financial processes and ease the burden of dealing with external contacts. PayMentor at *www.paymentor.com* is a five-step billing and collection service which monitors the whole accounts receivable cycle to intercept customer problems before they become debt-collection problems. For a small fee (£25 at the time of writing) businesses can submit up to 100 invoices into the system each month. PayMentor then emails reminders to customers and deals with subsequent transactions.

Credit Reports, at *www.creditreports.co.uk*, will fax information about any limited company's credit rating (including company profit and loss statements, balance sheets covering the last three years and details of company directors) and indicate the level of risk the company represents.

Government tax initiatives

The government wants to make tax matters simpler for small businesses. In November 2000 the Chancellor proposed several changes to the tax system, which it was hoped would provide a modern environment in which business can thrive. These measures, which were under consultation at the time of writing, included:

• simplifying and modernising the legislation concerning corporate debt, financial instruments and foreign exchange gains and losses
• clarifying the tax treatment for new limited liability partnerships
• clarifying the changes to the treatment of capital gains of companies introduced in the Finance Act 2000.

A package of tax initiatives to help small businesses was unveiled in March 2001. The proposals (currently under consultation) include:

• increasing the VAT threshold to £54,000 with the intention of helping 8,000 of the smallest businesses to escape the VAT net
• an optional flat-rate scheme for small businesses with a taxable turnover of under £100,000, enabling them to avoid having to account internally for VAT on all their purchases and sales. Instead, VAT might be calculated as a percentage of taxable turnover
• allowing small businesses with a taxable turnover of under £100,000 immediate entry to the annual accounting regime, instead of having to wait until one year after registration
• introducing a new consolidated SME taxable turnover level of £600,000 to help larger SMEs. This should allow an additional 40,000 traders to improve their cash flow
• raising the upper level of the entry threshold for the annual accounting scheme to £600,000. This should enable at least 100,000 businesses to file VAT returns annually instead of quarterly.

The Chancellor also proposed reducing tax compliance costs for life insurance companies that invest in venture capital limited partnerships, in order to encourage more of them to provide equity finance to SMEs through the medium of limited partnerships. Venture capital is discussed in Chapter 9. For more information about the government's proposals, see *A Review of Small Business Taxation* on the IR★ web site.

In addition to these initiatives, the government hopes to make it easier for people to decipher tax regulations. The Tax Law Rewrite project aims to make over 6,000 pages of tax law clearer. This involves the PAYE Regulations being rewritten as part of a first Income Tax Bill, which will be put before Parliament in November 2002. A second Income Tax Bill should follow in November 2003, to cover trading, property and savings and investment income. It is intended that the Tax Law Rewrite project will continue, regardless of which government is in power.

Tax relief on research and development

Innovation – the successful development of new ideas – is recognised by the government to boost productivity, open up new markets and benefit the economy. The IR offers tax relief on research and development (R&D) projects in order to stimulate investment in innovation. R&D allowances are a form of tax relief which enable SMEs to immediately write off all their spending on R&D against their income. They were formerly known as scientific research allowances when launched in 1945 to help rebuild Britain's economy after the war.

R&D tax credits were introduced in 2001. This means that companies can deduct 150 per cent (instead of 100 per cent) of any qualifying R&D expenditure when they calculate their taxable profits. Companies that do not make a profit can surrender their qualifying R&D losses and claim a cash payment of £24 for every £100 of qualifying R&D expenditure.

SMEs can claim R&D tax credits if they spend at least £25,000 per year on qualifying R&D. To qualify as an SME, a company must have:

- fewer than 250 employees
- an annual turnover of less than £25m and/or an annual balance sheet total of less than £17m
- less than 25 per cent of its capital or voting rights owned by a larger company or companies.

Companies that have not yet started trading can also claim R&D tax credits.

Costs that qualify for R&D tax credits are: employing staff to carry out the R&D, consumable stores used in the R&D, and certain subcontracting costs. R&D undertaken within a state-aided project (a government grant, for example) does not qualify for tax credits, as does any R&D project financed by a company that will not ultimately own the intellectual property rights.

For more information contact the IR.

The advice in this chapter should help you to put your finances in order. The following chapter covers methods of raising funds and encouraging investment in your company.

Chapter 8

Valuing a company

In order to raise money, you have to know what your company is worth. Similarly, if you are planning to expand your existing operation by acquiring another business you need to be able to put an accurate figure on the value of your proposed acquisition.

Several financial methods are used by valuation experts – usually accountancy firms – to assess the worth of a company. The combination deployed will depend upon the type of business. Added to this are other less tangible factors, such as 'goodwill', the power of a brand name or the age of a business, which can add or subtract value.

Many valuations are arrived at by comparing similar companies in the same industry. The problem is that perceptions of value change all the time within the investment field. For example, in 1999 dotcom companies were considered to be high-growth, high-yield businesses, and were valued at levels that far exceeded their eventual performance. Those that managed to stay in business are now worth a third or less of those initial valuations.

Financial valuation tools

The accepted valuation methods are described below. It is common to use more than one finance-based method and also to take into account other factors to build up a complete picture of a company.

Price/earnings ratio

The price/earnings (P/E) ratio is used to value businesses with a profitable track record. It represents the value of a business divided by its after-tax profits and is arrived at by comparing a business with like businesses in the same industry or commercial sector. The financial pages of newspapers give P/E ratios for quoted companies. Quoted companies traditionally have a higher P/E ratio – about 50 per cent higher than unquoted companies.

Several factors contribute to a higher P/E ratio. For example:

- the ability to demonstrate future profit growth which will add to the company's value in the next 12 months
- having regular earnings from guaranteed sources
- supplying a necessary part to a growth industry.

True profit needs to be calculated carefully. A company may present a rosy picture of increased profit in the future, but it is necessary to look at any additional costs that may accrue in order to achieve growth. For example, a business that increases its profits by acquiring a greater market segment may need to borrow more to finance new staff and make non-achieving staff redundant, or to invest in new plant and equipment or new technology.

Calculating the P/E ratio should ideally be undertaken by a professional, such as an accountant, who is used to putting a value on companies. Companies that do their own accounting may use inappropriate methods, resulting in calculations showing an artificial level of profit. Once an accurate P/E ratio has been fixed, a business should investigate ways to cut costs. Potential profit could be higher than it appears at first glance because reducing expenses such as overheads, procurement, salaries and shareholder payments may cut costs. For advice on running a business more effectively, see Chapter 4.

Once the P/E ratio is calculated and the true worth of your company established, you can use these figures to raise money via loans or investment (see Chapter 9), go public (sell your shares to the public via the open stock market), merge with another company or sell the company.

Assets

Calculating assets is a method that is particularly appropriate for companies that are rich in tangible assets – for example, a coach company with a fleet of vehicles, a manufacturing company with high-value stock, or a property company with housing.

The Net Book Value (NBV) of the assets that appear in the company's accounts must be ameliorated by taking account of the depreciation in value of those assets (particularly vehicles or old stock which has not been shifted) and any debts that have to be written off. If the business is failing, the assets will have to be sold at a knock-down price, it will be harder to call in outstanding debts, and staff who are laid off will have to be compensated. All of this will devalue the business.

Discounted cashflow

This method is applied to stable businesses with long-term prospects. It is based upon the sum of dividends forecast over a very long period (usually about 20 years into the future), plus a residual value at the end of the calculated period. It is highly complex because each dividend over the 20 years is calculated using a discount interest rate which projects the value of monies over the long term.

This would be the preferred method if, say, you were acquiring an old-established company whose operations would complement your own business. However, bolting on a business of this kind could lead to additional costs which may affect the value of your company. It may have to be re-engineered, for example, or require a massive injection of technology. This is the time to call in business consultants who can advise you on how to restructure and invest for maximum effect.

Other valuation factors

Many other factors which are unrelated to a business's financial performance can influence the value of a company.

Industry rules of thumb

A 'catch-all' method is used to calculate the value of businesses that are dependent on more than just profit. For example, the old-established business you seek to acquire might not make any money at all, but it could have a well-known brand name which you could add to your stable of products to give them credibility. It may have a high turnover or a large number of customers but need better management and a better pricing structure. Or it may have sales outlets in areas where you cannot get established.

> **The shoe company**
> A small shoe manufacturer which made children's shoes wanted to expand its range but found it difficult to break into the adult shoe market – particularly women's shoes. It decided to acquire another shoe manufacturer which had a brand profile in the women's marketplace, but was not making enough profit due to a poor pricing structure and having to pay over the odds for materials. The children's shoe manufacturing company was able to build on that brand profile and, by re-pricing and promoting the range, achieved a significant market presence. It also switched to its own suppliers, which were much cheaper, without compromising on quality, and as a result made greater profits.

These factors can affect the value of a company:

- **long-established business** Companies that have lasted a long time – say, 100 years – are respected for their staying power. However, if the management structure of such a company is so fossilised that it would cost a fortune to re-engineer it and install different management, it may not be worth buying
- **brand names** Well-known brands have kudos, and can be worth a lot. Alternatively a company's brands may be strong but a poor pricing structure might mean that they do not make any profit. Buyers should be wary of suppliers overcharging for ingredients or components
- **intellectual property/creative dynamism** A company with a track record of coming up with innovative ideas that it cannot successfully develop may look worthless on paper. However, a buyer could act as an incubator for that business and help get concepts off the drawing board (see page 46). This might involve considerable expense for the buyer
- **good business relationships** An old-established company may have excellent relationships with suppliers, customers and lending institutions. It can take years to achieve that kind of credibility, so this sort of company may be worth buying into

- **key personnel** A company may be totally reliant on certain employees for all its goodwill, sales, accounting skills, research and development. If these key staff leave, the company is effectively worthless. This constitutes a risky situation for buyers
- **too many overseas sales** This type of company is at the mercy of exchange-rate fluctuations. Investing in a switch to e-tailing might make it less vulnerable (see Chapter 5). The buyer would have to offset any investment in technology against the company's value on paper
- **no back-up systems** If important data is mishandled and a company has no back-up systems, IT specialists may have to put in a great deal of effort to retrieve and/or duplicate data. This could be too much hard work for very little return
- **no forward planning or research and development** If a company lacks the resources or infrastructure to generate or develop creative ideas, it could be advantageous for it to purchase another company with the wherewithal to see projects through from the drawing board to finished product. This can be successful if the acquired organisation complements the parent company and can handle the increased workload. For example, a CD manufacturer could choose to buy a recording artist's company which knows the trends in the music industry, signs up the artists and knows how to market the end product. That way, the CD manufacturer is potentially assured of constant work.

The radio station

A radio station in the Midlands put in a bid for another radio station in the north-west. Everything looked promising but when the former undertook a survey of the listener profile of the latter, it became clear that the majority of people who tuned in were loyal to a handful of the station's presenters, while only a very small percentage of them were interested in the station's overall style and genre. These findings prompted a re-think. The cost of tying the popular presenters down to new contracts was calculated, and revealed to be substantial. In the end, the Midlands radio station decided that buying the other company would not be a profitable exercise and the bid was shelved.

Shapers, adapters and reactors

When determining the value of a company, the ethos and approach of the business that is being valued may carry some weight. A company's worth may be influenced by whether it is proactive or reactive.

Franchee Harmon, the director of PricewaterhouseCoopers, identifies three types of companies:

- **shapers** – companies that actively go out and influence the market to make it move in a certain direction
- **adapters** – essentially, those that watch the shapers. Adapters allow shapers to take the initial risk and then try to be the fastest followers
- **reactors** – companies that think: 'The business is under threat, everybody has moved and I haven't. So now what do I do?' These companies are always the last to act, and often completely miss out on market and other opportunities.

These three types apply to old-economy businesses as well as the high-technology world. If you are interested in developing your business then you have to be a shaper, or at the very least, an adapter. Staying in the game means getting the ball and running with it, not just waiting for it to come to you. For example, the technology press have stressed the significance of building a value-added relationship with customers, and with this in mind many successful e-businesses have kept one step ahead of the market by creating personalised services for e-shoppers (see page 55).

Valuing e-businesses

The rise of e-business – signified by global markets, Internet trading and converging technologies – has meant that valuations have become increasingly difficult to accomplish. How *do* accountants calculate the value of a business which can literally say, 'London today – tomorrow the world' merely by creating a web site? There are no certainties anymore. Fashions, opinions and perceived needs all change rapidly. Global markets add to the sheer scale of fickleness in the buying public. If 28 million people in the USA can stop using the Internet in one year (see page 78), then whole marketplaces could collapse overnight. Many small companies which built up businesses e-tailing to the world lost large amounts of money due to the vagaries of Internet trading (discussed in Chapter 5).

It is easy to understand how financiers became caught up in the dotcom fiasco. But the hysteria of yesterday has now become tempered with caution. Today, specialist valuers can place far more accurate values on e-business companies. These companies, often known as incubators (see page 46), have re-invented the methodologies by which companies are valued and applied new systems to the present environment. For example, PricewaterhouseCoopers has created a framework it calls the High-tech Toolkit. This is a valuation system combined with new software which is designed to meet the needs of high-tech companies that operate in unfamiliar or uncertain markets. Special techniques allow businesses to monitor the development of the environment in which they operate and adjust a company's value accordingly. The Toolkit is also promoted as a management learning tool. Flexible new valuation methodologies such as the Toolkit suit the 'shifting sands' nature of e-business.

Any company thinking of purchasing another company that lives by the Internet should bear the following in mind:

- the safest Internet businesses are the ones that serve existing, healthy markets, selling consumer items for which there is already an established need (such as books and CDs), and not the companies that are trying to convince the world to try something new
- dotcom companies should be subjected to the same financial scrutiny as any other company and should be bound by the same simple rules. So if the income of a business exceeds expenditure it is probably a well-run company with prospects.
- if someone presents you with an idea for an Internet start-up company, first ask where the revenue is going to come from. The days of web sites making money purely from advertising are long gone. Unless a web site can generate hard sales or attract potential customers it is not viable
- do not be tempted to buy a dotcom company that deals in a business which is totally foreign to you. Stick to your core business. If the Internet company's activities are related to your existing business, or complement it, then you are more likely to be able to manage it effectively

- take advice from e-business experts. Large accountancy firms and management consultancies have divisions which deal specifically with high-tech business developments and expansions.

E-businesses should attempt to create added value to their own companies as they progress. They have, at their fingertips, the ability to monitor constantly the marketplace in which they operate, to review opportunities created by technological developments and to collect data about their customers' needs. For advice on strengthening your company's position in the marketplace see Chapter 6.

Those who attempt to value e-businesses will attach the highest value to companies that are shapers (see page 126). However, the valuers have to understand the technology sufficiently to be able to know whether it is going to work or not. Being good with figures and having a solid grounding in management techniques is no longer enough, particularly if you are trying to put a value on an e-business or trying to work out how much added value extra technology will bring to a company that has previously not invested in computers.

Considerations before buying a business

If you are contemplating buying a business, you need to ask the following questions:

- Does the company have to be sold (in other words, does the owner have no alternative)? If so, this may make it easier for you to bring down the asking price.
- Is the vendor under any time pressure (i.e. does the business need to be sold by a certain date in order for the vendor to emigrate, start another business or retire)? If so, this may be to your advantage, provided time pressure is not an issue for you.
- Is the main reason for selling the owner's financial needs, for example the need for cash to pay for retirement? Or does the business have problems, such as a disappearing market or no money for reinvestment? If the business is in trouble because of external factors, you will inherit the same problems.

- Do the existing management hope to stay with the company? The loss of key staff can be damaging. Old hands are often a source of valuable knowledge.
- Has the vendor freely given information or is he/she hiding any essential detail from you? For example, an owner who realises that his or her company has lost a significant amount of goodwill over the last few years due to inefficiency or poor customer service may be reluctant to give you that information.
- What is the competition? If a company is struggling and looking to be bought out, the reason could be that the competition is too fierce. Any attempt to gain back a significant market share would require a huge amount of investment in technology and people. If, however, the competition is limited and the company is struggling simply because of a lack of cash and poor management skills then the business might be easy to knock into shape, and could be a good investment.
- What do industry experts, financial advisers and employees think of the company? The opinions of those in the industry count for a lot. You can find out from industry gurus whether the company you propose to buy has any goodwill or a sound reputation. Financial advisers will be able to tell you about the financial health of the company and predict future scenarios, while the existing employees will be able to tell you whether they are happy, unhappy, loyal, enthusiastic or dejected by the company's methods of operation, business relationships and future prospects.

Before attempting to buy a company, seek professional help in order to value that company correctly. A number of non-financial factors will come into play (see 'Industry rules of thumb', page 123). Try to identify where savings can be made and profits can be increased. Once you are armed with sufficient knowledge you will be able to calculate correctly how much that business is worth to you and negotiate from a position of strength.

The bargaining process

At the end of the day, a business is worth what it is worth to the buyer. A buyer will have his or her own agenda and will know what the addition of another business will do for the core activity. It is not advisable to disclose the other company's strategic significance to your plans. If the seller is aware how much his or her business is worth to you, then the power is in his or her hands. An accountant will advise you to weigh the potential value of a company against whatever risks and costs you incur.

Bear in mind the following points during negotiations to buy a business.

- After careful calculation, arrive at a minimum and maximum figure for the purchase of the company. The minimum figure is what you would like to buy the company for and the maximum figure is the most you could afford to pay for it without making a loss.
- Make your first offer with the minimum figure.
- Do not accept the vendor's figures.
- Your offer should be made in writing through your solicitors. This will require a correct response. Be sure to highlight the positive aspects of the offer and explain what being bought out will mean for the company you are seeking to purchase – for example, investment in technology, saved jobs, new market possibilities or new product development.
- Give a deadline for reply.
- Negotiate until you arrive at a mutually agreeable price.
- Let your professional advisers (e.g. accountants, lawyers) finalise the purchase.

Throughout the negotiation period, it is vital to communicate with employees and where possible reassure them that their positions are secure, ensuring that the process is as stress-free as possible. If you envisage job losses in the long term, you should make your intentions clear and must give affected employees as much help as possible, allowing them time off to attend interviews, offering redundancy payments where appropriate and employing them in your company if possible. The DTI* publishes a useful booklet entitled *Employment Rights on the Transfer of an Undertaking*.

Chapter 9

Obtaining finance

This chapter looks at ways of raising funds and encouraging investment in your business, including getting a grant.

Finding new money

However you raise money, the criteria are the same. Investors will
want to know whether you can show a clear path to profitability.
They will want to see your business growth plan, and be confident
that:

- you have control over your costs
- you have identified and penetrated the market
- your supply and distribution networks are in place
- you know the value of your company.

Chapter 1 covers the business plan, and establishing the value of a
company is described in Chapter 8. Below we outline the different
ways of obtaining finance.

Venture capital

Venture capital provides long-term, committed share capital to help
unquoted companies grow and succeed. It can help if you are
expanding, buying into a business, buying out a division of your
parent company or revitalising a company. Venture capital may not
be appropriate if you are a very small company seeking to expand,
although you could approach the 20 per cent of venture capital
firms that are interested in investing smaller amounts. If you have

recently started up you might be better off approaching a business angel (see page 136).

The UK venture capital industry is the largest and most developed in Europe, and second only to that of the United States in terms of world importance. Nearly £23 billion has been invested by venture capital firms in more than 16,500 businesses since 1985. About 80 per cent of venture capital firms invest over £100,000 per company per year. The average annual investment in expansion financings is about £1 million, and investment in management buy-outs and buy-ins usually totals about £5 million.

A survey entitled *The Economic Impact of Venture Capital in the UK 1998*, undertaken by Bannock Consulting and jointly sponsored by the British Venture Capital Association (BVCA)* and PricewaterhouseCoopers, produced statistics which demonstrate the positive effect of venture capital:

- the number of people employed in venture-backed companies in 1998 increased by 24 per cent compared to a national growth rate of 1.3 per cent
- on average, venture-backed companies achieved exceptional growth in 1998. Sales rose by 40 per cent, pre-tax profits increased by 24 per cent, exports grew by 44 per cent and investment increased by 34 per cent
- 95 per cent of the companies in the survey would not have existed, or would have grown less rapidly, without venture capital
- 56 per cent of companies rated venture capital firms as superior to their commercial banks in terms of effectiveness and commitment.

Many of the businesses that benefited from venture capital in 1998 were dotcom companies and so the statistics might not look quite so impressive today. However, the failure of many Internet start-ups has probably worked to the advantage of established businesses that wish to expand with the assistance of venture capital, because investors are now more inclined to invest in companies with a proven track record, rather than in exotic start-ups which promise much and deliver little.

Venture capital schemes

Three schemes enable investors to receive tax relief for minority investment in new, full-risk shares in small, independent higher-risk companies:

- the Enterprise Investment Scheme (EIS) – for individuals investing directly
- the Venture Capital Trust Scheme (VCT) – for individuals investing in venture capital trusts which in turn invest in such shares
- the Corporate Venturing Scheme (CVS) – for companies investing directly.

In March 2001, the government proposed relaxing some of the qualifying rules of these schemes in order to enable more small entrepreneurial companies to benefit. The Inland Revenue (IR)★ can supply booklets and brief guides on each scheme.

Attracting venture capital

In order to raise venture capital for your company you have to select the right firm to approach with your business plan. The BVCA's *Directory of Members* gives details of member companies and their investment preferences. It also includes the names of some of the companies in which venture capital firms have invested.

The type of investment that you require depends very much on the stage of development your company has reached.

- **Seed financing** This is an injection of money into a concept. It occurs when a great deal of research and development must be undertaken before a business or product can be launched in a market. Not many investors are interested in this type of financing since it is thought to require too much support and supervision. Also, most seed finances are too small to be attractive to large venture capital companies. If you are at this stage, you should approach a business angel instead (see page 136).
- **Start-up financing** This type of finance suits businesses which are beyond the concept stage and are either in the process of being set up or have been running for a while but need investment to develop properly. About 10 per cent of financings each year are in start-ups.

- **Early-stage financing** This is generally regarded as appropriate for companies that have been trading for a while and have good prospects, but have not yet gone into profit. This accounts for 10 per cent of financings each year.
- **Expansion financing** This is the big area of investment, accounting for about 50 per cent of financings each year. It applies to established companies which need to grow and expand.
- **Management buy-out** This significant area of finance accounts for 20 per cent of investment each year. It helps existing management buy out a company or acquire a significant shareholding in a business that they manage.
- **Other types of financing** Different forms of financing – such as management buy-in, rescue/turnaround and refinancing bank debt – are also available but represent an insignificant amount of investment each year.

Once you have found a selection of venture capital firms that are interested in your business sector and the size of your company, you need to put together a detailed proposal and business plan. For information on how to go about this, see Chapter 1. The BVCA's *Directory of Members* lists fee-charging advisers who can help you present your case properly to the right people.

Venture capital vs bank loans
Some companies prefer to get a loan from a bank because they like to be in control of their expansion and do not want to be dictated to by investors who might want to accelerate growth in order to get a decent return on their investment. However, venture capital offers certain advantages, as outlined by the BVCA (see below).

Comparison of venture capital with senior debt (loan)	
Venture capital	**Senior debt**
Medium to long term.	Short to long term.
Committed until 'exit'.	Not likely to be committed if the safety of the loan is threatened. Overdrafts are payable on demand; loan facilities may be payable on demand if the covenants are not met.

Venture capital	Senior debt
Provides a solid, flexible, capital base to meet your future growth and development plans.	A useful source of finance if the debt to equity ratio is conservatively balanced and the company has a good cash flow.
Good for cash flow, as capital repayment dividend and interest costs (if relevant) are tailored to the company's needs and to what it can afford.	Requires a good cash flow to service interest and capital repayments.
Returns to the venture capital investor depend on the business' growth and success. The more successful the company is, the better the returns received by all investors.	Returns depend on the company continuing to service its interest costs and maintaining the value of the assets on which the debt is secured.
If the business fails, venture capital investors rank alongside other share-holders, after the banks and other lenders, and stand to lose their investment.	If the business fails, the lender generally has first call on the company's assets.
If the business runs into difficulties, the venture capital firm will work hard to ensure that the company is turned around.	If the business appears likely to fail, the lender could put it into receivership in order to safeguard its loan. The lender could also make the owner/manager bankrupt if personal guarantees have been given.

Business angels

If you have a business concept you want to develop, or hope to diversify or expand your company, a business angel may be the answer. These are individuals who generally invest smaller amounts than venture capital firms and prefer companies at an early stage of development – some 40 per cent of business angel investments in 1998-9 were in smaller companies seeking to expand.

Whereas venture capital firms are really just interested in making an investment and do not want to get involved with the company, the typical business angel is a combination of mentor and investor who is prepared to help maximise his or her investment by means of practical intervention. Many business angels are retired businesspeople with spare cash, successful owner/managers who like to assist in the development of businesses unrelated to their own, or accountants with the financial acumen to spot ventures that are likely to succeed.

Many business angels invest under the Enterprise Investment Scheme (see page 133), as tax incentives are available if the company requiring investment meets EIS criteria. For the companies concerned, involvement with a business angel can prove beneficial later on – many venture capital firms look more kindly on requests for larger investments from companies that have formed a relationship with a business angel.

During the 1990s the number of business angel networks nearly tripled. According to research by the University of Southampton, in 1999 registered business angels invested £109 million in 1,085 registered companies. However, following the failure of many dotcom start-ups, business angels have come down to earth and developed a tougher approach to investment.

Local agents of the National Business Angels Network (NBAN)* organise investor clubs and company presentations which are attended by business angels who are willing to talk about their experiences and how the system works. The free *Sources of Business Angel Capital Directory*, published by the BVCA, lists nearly 50 business angel networks.

Getting a grant

Over 800 grants provided by national organisations or European Union sources are available in the UK. An additional 3,000 grants are provided by economic development units, Enterprise Agencies, local authorities and other bodies. A thriving business has grown up in grant consultancy – companies that help UK businesses find their way through the maze of paperwork and application procedures. A grant is sometimes not really a grant (which should be a gift of cash) but a 'soft loan' (see below).

Types of grant

Several forms of grant exist.

Direct grant
This is a straightforward donation of cash for a variety of business activities which does not have to be paid back. Typically, an amount of about 50 per cent of the project's cost is proffered.

Repayable grant
This type of grant is offered to fund a project on the assumption that it will be repaid (without any interest) if the project succeeds. There is no repayment if the project fails.

Soft loan
This is a type of loan which is more generous than a bank loan. It could be interest-free or rate-reduced, or be over a longer term, involving a capital repayment holiday or a reduction in collateral requirements. Ultimately it must be paid back.

Equity finance
Not to be confused with venture capital (see page 131), this is where an individual or organisation chooses to inject money into a business in return for a share of it, but does not expect interest payments on the loan or repayment of the loan itself. It is an expression of confidence in the future of a business and reflects an expectation that the share in the business may, eventually, reap some dividends.

How much money can you get?

The amount of grant you are entitled to depends upon several factors:

- the purpose of the grant (what you want to do with it)
- the size of your company (small can sometimes be better)
- the area in which you operate (there are special grants for areas of high unemployment, rural areas, areas where large industries have closed down and so on)
- your turnover
- your industry (some are excluded – see 'Businesses excluded from grant schemes', opposite)
- how much money is available (you will almost certainly need to provide some of the cost of a project or even match a grant sum).

Grants for different purposes

Grants fall into various categories, depending on their function.

Research and development grants
These grants offer between 30 and 50 per cent of the total project cost. Such costs can include salaries, related capital expenditure, consultancy, intellectual property insurance, consumables and some portion of total overheads.

Training grants
These grants meet between 20 and 50 per cent of training costs. Some industries are particularly favoured (such as engineering), and priority may be given to particular cases – for example, retraining employees who have been made redundant from large industries which collapsed (such as mining). Soft loans can be obtained by smaller businesses to cover up to 80 per cent of training costs.

Capital grants for investment
These are on offer as part of job creation programmes in areas of high unemployment. Grant levels range from 5 per cent to 25 per cent, which equates to about £2,500–£7,000 for each employee with a new job.

Export grants

The amount of these grants varies depending upon the activity that requires a subsidy. This can be anything from setting up an export business, consultancy and export trips abroad, to joint venture financing.

Infrastructure grants

These are grants for areas which have suffered an economic decline. They cover not just regions but specific industries, such as fishing, and are designed to assist in the formation of new markets or alternative employment.

Advisory service grants

These grants contribute up to 50 per cent of the cost of consultancy services for specific approved projects.

Miscellaneous grants

These grants cover many aspects of business life and are offered with special interest rates by a large number of organisations. The Royal British Legion,* for example, offers grants to help ex-servicemen and women set up in business or develop an existing business. Shell LiveWIRE* and the Prince's Trust* offer grants and soft loans to young businesspeople. The government offers grants to businesses that employ or benefit disabled people, and the Arts Council* finances artists and craftspeople who are in the process of developing companies. Other grants are available for the development of businesses in rural areas and woodland and nature reserves, and to help farmers diversify without abandoning the land. For information contact the Woodland Trust,* the Forestry Commission* and the Countryside Agency.*

Businesses excluded from grant schemes

Certain types of industries are excluded from receiving any grant from any source:

- banks
- financial services
- insurance companies
- estate agencies.

Industries which are numerous in the EU – such as shipbuilding, coal mining, fisheries, agriculture, food and drink manufacturers and textile manufacturers – are generally not considered for grants from any source, although sometimes a special case might be made for a small company with specialist skills. For example, a small firm making rare forms of textiles may qualify for a grant from arts and crafts sources.

Companies that have a purely local presence – such as a local newspaper – are unlikely to be considered for national grants, but might qualify for local grants. Retail businesses are rarely eligible unless the company meets a specialist criterion, such as providing new jobs for an area of high unemployment. Any grant linked to a specific locality will not apply to businesses outside that area – so grants for urban regeneration are not available to rural businesses, for example.

Sources of grants

Grants are available from a number of government and local sources.

The European Union (EU)

The EU is the main source of grants and other funds, and administers a diverse range of schemes through various channels. However, compared to local, regional and national grants these funds are difficult to access, the application criteria are complicated and the process can be very slow. Also, it is not unknown for funds to be discontinued while businesses are in the middle of preparing an application. For more information, first access the European Union web site at *europa.eu.int/comm/secretariat_general/sgc/into_subv/index_en.htm*

UK government

Most EU grants are administered through the government departments and agencies listed below. National and regional funds are also available from these bodies.

- Department of Trade and Industry (DTI)★
- Department for Education and Employment (DfEE)★

- Department of the Environment, Transport and the Regions (DETR)★
- Ministry of Agriculture, Fisheries and Food (MAFF)★
- Local Enterprise Development Unit (LEDU)★ (Northern Ireland)
- Industrial Development Board★ (Northern Ireland)
- Scottish Executive★
- Welsh Development Agency★
- The Countryside Agency★
- Industrial Research and Technology Unit (IRTU).★

Several hundred local authorities make a limited amount of funds available for business development, as do these locally based groups:

- Business Link★ (England)
- Small Business Service (SBS)★
- Enterprise Agencies – see page 16
- Training and Enterprise Councils (TECs) – see page 15
- Local Enterprise Companies (LECs) (Scotland) – see page 15
- Business Connect★ (Wales)
- Enterprise Trusts (Scotland) – see page 16
- Scottish Enterprise★
- Highlands & Islands Enterprise (HIE).★

Government initiatives

Government schemes that provide funds at the time of writing are listed below.

Phoenix Fund

The government created the Phoenix Fund★ in November 1999. This £30m fund is intended to encourage entrepreneurship in disadvantaged communities and groups. It includes the provision to plough more resources into Community Finance Initiatives (CFIs) so that these can, in turn, give more help to new and growing businesses. CFIs are local, non-profit organisations which lend smaller amounts to businesses that banks consider investment risks.

The Phoenix Fund comprises four elements:

- a development fund which promotes innovative ways of supporting enterprise in deprived areas
- a pilot network of volunteer mentors to assist pre- and early start-up businesses, through the Business Volunteer Mentoring Association (for more on mentors see page 43)
- a challenge fund to help resource Community Finance Initiatives
- loan guarantees to encourage commercial and charitable lending to Community Finance Initiatives.

In order to obtain financial assistance, the businesses supported by CFIs must be able to prove that they are viable and self-sustaining.

SBS Small Firms Loan Guarantee

This scheme guarantees loans from banks and other financial institutions for SMEs with viable business propositions which have tried and failed to obtain conventional loans because of a lack of security.

Loans are available for periods of between two and ten years on sums from £5,000 to £100,000 (or £250,000 if the business has been trading for more than two years). The Small Business Service (SBS)* guarantees 70 per cent of the loan (85 per cent if the business has been trading for more than two years). In return for the guarantee, the borrower pays the SBS a premium of 1.5 per cent a year on the outstanding amount of the loan. The premium is reduced to 0.5 per cent if the loan is taken at a fixed rate of interest.

To be eligible you must be a UK company with an annual turnover of no more than £1.5m (£3m if you are a manufacturer). Most of the major banks and some lending organisations are involved in the scheme. Contact the SBS for details.

SBS Smart Scheme

The SBS Smart Scheme provides grants to individuals and SMEs to review, research or develop technologies leading to the manufacture of commercial products. The following section outlines the help available in England. Scotland, Wales and Northern Ireland have their own initiatives, which are roughly similar, called smart

Scotland, smart Innovation Awards (Wales), and Innovation Into Success in Northern Ireland.

The doily-making machine

Paper doilies are used extensively by bakers' shops, hotel bars, restaurants and cafés. A small five-person company in Milton Keynes, with skills in general engineering, fabrication, machining and design developed a new doily-making machine with the help of a Smart Scheme award. Design and development of the machine took about three years. The new machine works three times faster than its predecessors, speeding product changes and minimising downtime and maintenance, while decreasing inventory and improving the quality of the finished product. On completion it was sold to a Belgian paper converting company. The company went on to sell two more, both to overseas customers. Thanks to the Smart award, the company is now looking forward to a profitable exporting future.

The following grants are available.

- **Technology reviews** Grants of up to £2,500 for individuals and SMEs (with fewer than 250 employees) towards the cost of expert reviews (i.e. analysis of how a company can improve performance in many areas).
- **Technology studies** Grants of up to £5,000 for individuals and SMEs (with fewer than 250 employees) to help identify technological opportunities that may lead to innovative products and processes.
- **Micro projects** Grants of up to £10,000 to help individuals and micro-firms (with fewer than ten employees) which are developing low-cost product prototypes and processes involving technical advances and/or novelty.
- **Feasibility studies** Grants of up to £45,000 for individuals and small firms (with fewer than 50 employees) undertaking feasibility studies into innovative technologies.
- **Development projects** Grants of up to £150,000 for SMEs (with fewer than 250 employees) undertaking development projects.

- **Exceptional development projects** Grants of up to £450,000 for SMEs (with fewer than 250 employees) undertaking a small number of exceptionally high-cost development projects.

For more information about the Smart Scheme, contact the SBS.

The fish bait breeder

Marine worms are a valuable bait for sea angling, but until a few years ago they had a limited breeding season. A Smart award-winning company in Northumberland developed a technique for considerably extending the worm breeding season, enabling all-year-round availability for anglers and also making redundant the need for environmentally destructive bait digging on UK shores.

The company used a first Smart award to investigate scientifically the worms' breeding season. As a result, it developed two methods of manipulating the breeding season. A second Smart award allowed the company to refine the techniques commercially. The company has since more than doubled sales and production, and has increased employment by 50 per cent so that it currently employs over 20 people. With the benefit of further Smart awards, they have begun to cultivate other species such as lugworms, opening up worldwide opportunities for exports in the bait market and for mainstream aquaculture feedstuffs.

Other initiatives

Some other government grants are currently available.

- SMEs can benefit from a range of regionally based schemes aimed at new and small businesses which are supported by European Structural Funds. These funds promote competitiveness throughout Europe. Details of all European funds available for business can be obtained through the national government agencies listed on pages 140–1.
- An Enterprise Grant is a one-off financial assistance package for small and medium-sized enterprises investing in projects in the Assisted Areas and Enterprise Grant Areas of the English regions. The Regional Selective Assistance scheme aims to attract investment and create or safeguard jobs in the Assisted Areas via grants for larger projects with fixed capital costs of over £500,000. For

more information, contact the regional organisations listed on pages 140–1.

- The DfEE* operates the New Deal, which provides financial support towards salary and training costs for companies employing young and long-term unemployed people.

Finding out about grants

If you are planning to enter the world of grant applications, you need to keep abreast of what is available. There are several ways to do this.

You could trawl through the many web sites which offer finance information. The Enterprise Zone at *www.enterprisezone.org.uk* offers links to 20 grant sites along with other useful links. The DTI* has the latest information on government initiatives. Its web site at *www.dti.co.uk* is easy to access. The EU web sites also provide information, but are not so easy to find your way around. For details about EU funding contact *europa.eu.int/comm/secretariat_general/sgc/into_subv/ index_en.htm* or look up *www.cec.org.uk/directry/eu-inst.htm* for EU information sources.

Another route is to contact a grant advisory and application service. This is now offered by many consultancies; however, it is best to approach only those which feature in government web site links. A consultancy's appearance on official web pages should not be taken as a firm recommendation but is, nevertheless, an indication that the company is deemed to be reputable.

In addition, several publications deal with grants. Your local reference library should have a copy of *Grants and aid for business: a practical guide to the financial support and advisory services available to companies from central government, local authorities and other organisations.*

Applying for grants

The funds are limited. The applicants are many. You have to compete for a grant, and that means using your common sense and more than a little business acumen when it comes to filling in application forms. You will need to have done your sums and should be able to supply the grant provider with full details of how you propose to use the grant. You may find the advice in the box overleaf useful.

Maximising your chances of getting a grant

1 Research thoroughly what types of grant are available.
2 Note that you cannot start on any project unless an application for a grant has been made.
3 Your application must be for a specific project.
4 Apply for a grant as early as possible, particularly in the case of new schemes.
5 Make sure that your grant application matches the objectives of the awarding body, which will be clearly laid out in the relevant literature.
6 Highlight the long-term benefits of your project in your application, stating if there are particular benefits to science or the community.
7 Upgrade your company's business plan (see Chapter 1) – the awarding body will want to see it. You should draw up a plan that relates specifically to the project for which you need funding.
8 Make clear how much the funds matter to you, and explain that if you do not get assistance the project will not go ahead.
9 Ensure that you have matching funds. It is rare for a grant to cover more than 50 per cent of a project. You must have the other 50 per cent guaranteed.
10 Ask for advice from the awarding body or from the many grant consultants that have sprung up in recent years. The more you know about the grant system, the better.

Other forms of support

Many alternative forms of support are available that can save money for businesses, such as advice, information, training and group membership. Some benefactor organisations will help companies formulate business plans, create proper accounts, select staff and provide IT training, offering services free of charge which would cost a great deal in the commercial world. You can find out about these organisations through the government bodies listed on pages 140–1.

Chapter 10

Expanding your business

Sometimes growth cannot be achieved organically within your company for a variety of reasons:

- you are in a fast-developing business sector and you need to grow apace to keep a hold on the marketplace
- you need to develop a new business area which will require more space/new staff/new equipment/retraining of existing staff and so on
- you need to diversify into a different marketplace that requires a new approach but also want to maintain your existing business, which is doing well
- you need to have a presence in another town/region/country
- you need to take control of your supplies of raw materials in order to be absolutely sure about quality, reliability etc.
- you need to enlarge your customer base
- your existing management team has taken your original business into strong profit and could easily achieve the same with another business.

Any of the above reasons could propel you towards an 'instant' expansion, which can only be achieved by a merger, an acquisition or by creating a franchise (see page 152).

Whichever process you choose, it will be costly – probably a similar expense to expanding your existing company over a period of time. However, what you are buying is a measure of speed, and – if you pick the right option and company to merge with or acquire, or develop a franchise with the right ingredients – a quicker route to success.

Types of diversification

Some of the reasons for achieving quick growth have been outlined above. The definitions used for different types of expansion are:

- conglomerate diversification
- related diversification
- geographical diversification
- horizontal diversification
- vertical diversification.

You will need to understand these terms since they are likely to be used by banks and other lending institutions.

Conglomerate diversification

This term explains the acquisition of one or more unrelated companies by a business that majors in management and administration, on the grounds that it can run those companies better and achieve a greater profit than the current owners. For example, a small businessman or -woman might start out by acquiring another small business in order to run it more effectively without disrupting the needs of the first business. The profits generated could encourage the parent company to build up a small group of companies that do not relate to each other but, nevertheless, can be run comfortably by the same management group. Many large empires, such as Virgin and Hanson, started this way. In order to persuade a lender that you are capable of building up this sort of empire from scratch you would have to demonstrate a good management record and show that you can generate profit with your original business. For more information on drawing up a business plan see Chapter 1.

Related diversification

This describes what happens when a company capitalises on its name and reputation in order to acquire a company that is in a related, but not identical, business. For example, a fashion designer might build up a name as a clothes designer and then decide to diversify into cosmetics (deemed to be in the same marketplace). Since the fashion house would not possess the ability to manufacture perfume and face creams, it could either acquire a company that has the manufacturing capability or be acquired by a cosmetics

---

The Welsh conglomerate (conglomerate diversification)
A farm machinery hire business was set up by two brothers in Wales. It prospered and both brothers found that they enjoyed the challenge of management. The business was practically running itself when the brothers came upon the opportunity to buy a local wooden outdoor furniture company that was in need of investment and fresh management. Within a year they had turned the company around, introduced new lines and gained several contracts with major DIY stores and garden centres. With the management systems in place and new staff hired, the furniture company became self-sufficient and the brothers looked around for another company to add to their stable. They found it in the shape of a small glass factory, only 20 miles away from their other companies. The company made cheap glasses for the licensed trade and had run into trouble because of cutbacks on contracts by various breweries. The brothers were able to invest money in some new machinery which enabled the production process to diversify into more unusual ranges of drinking glasses. As a result they found new customers in upmarket gift shops and mail-order catalogues. The group comprises the three companies described above at the time of writing, but the brothers plan to look for another company to add to the group in another year or so.

---

manufacturer. To give an example on a much smaller scale, a local estate agency with a reputation for good service might acquire a reliable local building company in order to offer a comprehensive property maintenance and sales service to customers.

Geographical diversification

This is the acquisition of a presence, sales outlet or marketing platform by a company in another part of the UK or abroad. Inevitably different tastes, income levels, culture and standards will be encountered (see Chapter 6). This may mean that it would be more expensive for the original company to mount a special marketing campaign, use overseas agents and change products, than it would be for it to acquire a similar company in that area and use it as a means of expansion and a sales outlet. Retail empires such as Laura

---

The pet shop (related diversification)

Mr B runs a very successful pet shop in a large town in North Yorkshire. He became aware, by talking to his customers, that a large kennels and cattery (the only such establishment in the immediate vicinity) was up for sale due to the owner's impending retirement. Mr B had been looking for a way to expand his business interests and acquire a company for his daughter to run. She was a trained veterinary nurse but did not like the distressing side of her job and was not interested in running another pet shop. A kennels and cattery seemed ideal. The business in question was run from a large country house and made a modest profit. Mr B bought the company and his daughter has now expanded the business to include boarding for a variety of pets. She also runs other pet services such as grooming, dog training classes and weight management clinics for domestic pets, and rents out the grounds for dog, cat and horse shows. All of these initiatives have helped increase the profitability of the original company.

Ashley, Past Times and Index started small and developed by acquiring outlets around the UK. Other chains deliberately opened shops in certain areas because the local tastes and income levels were so markedly different from those in their own region that they were able to extend their range of products and thereby create a greater profit margin. Local newspapers are a good example of geographical diversification. Most local newspaper groups started off as one paper and then gradually expanded into other geographical areas by acquiring existing publications.

Horizontal diversification

This is the straightforward acquisition of like companies. For example, a shoe manufacturer might acquire another shoe manufacturing company so that he or she can instantly expand his or her companies' capacity, range of products, sales outlets and personnel.

Vertical diversification

There are two types of vertical diversification: 'backwards' and 'forwards'. These terms refer to a company acquiring another company

The textile manufacturer, importer and retailer (geographical diversification)

A textile company in Lancashire makes a small range of its own products but has diversified into importing cheap textiles from abroad, buying up ends of ranges and discontinued lines from other manufacturers and selling all these products through a sales outlet and mail-order catalogue. It aims its advertising at women who enjoy sewing and crafts and has an extensive customer base spread throughout the UK.

Through its mail-order company, the company pursues a policy of allowing potential customers to ask for samples of cloth (£1 for 10 small samples) so that they can see the cloth before they buy, and perhaps match up colours and textures. The company found that by far the largest percentage of samples was requested by customers in Kent, Surrey and Sussex and so reasoned that if it had a retail outlet in the south of England, it would probably attract a great deal of 'walk-in' custom. The company accordingly acquired an existing fabric retail business with a good supplier network, a healthy customer base and two sales outlets in Guildford and Canterbury.

that is either behind, or in front of it, in the supply chain. If a company that made lawnmowers acquired the company that supplied it with nuts and bolts, it would be said to be diversifying backwards. If the lawnmower company acquired the company which owned a chain of garden centres that sold its lawnmowers, it would be said to be diversifying forwards.

The preserves company (vertical diversification)

A small food manufacturing company in Scotland which makes preserves – jam, marmalade and curds – got so fed up with the erratic quality of the glass jars that came from its suppliers that it bought a glass factory. This was done mainly to ensure a regular supply of good-quality jars but also so that the company could supply other food manufacturers with containers.

The main routes to instant expansion are explained overleaf.

Acquisitions

This route probably offers the greatest chance of success if you are trying to expand quickly, but is likely to be the most costly. You will need to buy out the current owners of the company you wish to acquire and you will also need to pay for the name the company has built up and its existing net assets. Hopefully, all these costs will be more than rewarded by the target company's established goodwill, entry into a lucrative marketplace, established supply chains, good customer outlets, lack of outstanding debts, manufacturing or processing capabilities and experienced staff.

Mergers

This is a less expensive route than acquisition because, while acquisition usually means that you purchase total management control of the acquired company, merging generally leaves some management control in the hands of the company with which you are merging. There is usually a majority owner (your company) and a minority owner (the company you seek to merge with), and your company will be expected to inject some cash into the other company in order to rejuvenate it in certain areas. The lack of total management control is the reason why some mergers do not succeed. It can be difficult to find another management team that has exactly the same standards, aims and objectives as your own, and the resultant conflict can cost the company in missed opportunities and profits in the long run.

Franchising

A 'business-format franchise', as it is known, is basically the granting of a licence by one business (the franchiser) to another (the franchisee), which allows the franchisee to trade under the name of the franchiser's company. However, a franchise is more than just a business contract. It is a total package which consists of the company's ethos and business concept (what the company does, how it operates, its corporate identity, the product/service itself, the company's standards), an element of training for the franchisee so that he/she/they will be able to run the company to the necessary standards, and a facility for continuous advice, guidance and back-up. Typical examples of franchises include fast-food chains, dry-cleaners, restaurants and print shops.

The franchiser usually charges for the licence. The size of the fee depends upon the following factors:

- the value of the name of the company (whether it is well-known, has a good reputation, an established marketplace and so on)
- the solidity of the company (its financial track record, the length of time it has operated, its reliability etc.)
- whether the company has good supply chains that will service all franchisees equally well
- whether the franchiser is able to offer a good package of training, support and advice
- whether the franchiser is able to offer ongoing management supervision, quality control and good lines of communication
- whether the franchisee is able to be included in regional/national/international advertising campaigns by the franchiser
- whether the franchiser is able to provide for purchase of all the required equipment in good condition, and assist if necessary with the finding of premises, planning permissions, licences, shop layouts, refurbishments and stock levels
- whether the franchiser is able to minimise greatly any business risk to the franchisee in the operation of the business
- whether the franchisee has the benefit of the franchiser's specialist personnel in accounts, finance, research and development and other areas
- whether the franchisee has the benefit of the use of the franchiser's trade marks, patents, copyrights, formulae, product developments and any other new processes.

Any company considering the franchise route as a method of expansion needs to consult an expert about whether it is advisable to proceed. It should also seek help in putting together and valuing the package. The more advice you can get, the better informed you will be when it comes to making the final decision. The British Franchise Association (BFA)* can provide assistance. In addition, all the major banks have franchise experts who can give advice. They will expect to see roughly the same sort of material as they would if you were starting up a new business: i.e. evidence of experience, stability, financial security and the ability to cope financially during the first couple of years. Once you have collected all the information you need from the franchising company, you could ask your bank to help you draw up a business plan (see Chapter 1) or assist with whatever documentation is needed to process your application. Banks may charge for this service.

Some fundamental questions have to be answered before you can start naming prices or advertising your franchise to the hopeful franchisees. Banks in particular will want to ensure that your plan for a franchise empire satisfies their requirements.

It will help if you can meet the following criteria:

- you have experience of franchising
- you have successfully run a number of pilot schemes (see below) in a variety of locations
- you have investigated the marketplace thoroughly
- you can reassure franchisees that they will be investing in a business which has dealt with and resolved problems on a day-to-day basis
- you are able to adequately finance your activities during the first year of franchising
- your corporate structure and infrastructure are able to cope with growth of a franchise network
- you can provide audited accounts, and demonstrate that your financial position has not deteriorated since they were drawn up
- you can prove that you have suitable selection criteria for franchisees
- none of your senior executives has been involved in unsuccessful franchise ventures, or companies that have gone into liquidation or receivership.

It is important that you thoroughly research the question of franchising your business so that, when you approach your expert adviser and produce a business plan, you will be ready to run a pilot scheme.

Operating a pilot scheme

Experts advise that pilot schemes should preferably be run for at least 12 months, ideally in more than one location, in order to test the viability of your proposed franchise. Franchising is therefore not a quick expansion method. However, if, after taking advice, you consider that planning for growth after 12 months will suit your needs then perhaps the franchising option is for you.

If the pilot scheme works well, you can prepare to launch your network. Financial and business advisers will have been involved before the pilot scheme launch – now is the time to get lawyers to draw up the agreements. They should be experts in franchising. You will also need to draw up a prospectus to place before potential franchisees and decide your criteria for successful applicants.

When deciding on your requirements for franchisees, consider the following:

- What experience will you expect potential franchisees to have?
- Will you have a minimum/maximum age requirement?
- Will you require proof of good health?
- Will you require proof of financial security?
- Will you test aptitudes and skills?
- Are you looking for someone who will run the franchise on his or her own, or are you prepared to accept an absentee owner? If so, will you have a say in the manager/ess the owner employs?
- Does the potential franchisee understand the commitment required, the hours that need to be worked and the level of management control that your company will exercise?
- Does the applicant have the necessary specialist skills – i.e. a foreign language or engineering qualifications?

In addition to deciding the level of control you will have over applicants, you will also have to consider practicalities such as whether you will supply raw materials or stocks and set prices.

The BFA is the best place to go for detailed advice in the initial stages. It publishes a code of ethics which its members must adhere to. This comprises two documents – the *European Code of Ethics for Franchising* and the BFA's own 'extension and interpretation' of the code. You can also visit the web site of the Small Business Service (SBS).* *Buying a Franchise* is a booklet available from the SBS which can also be downloaded in PDF format from its web site.

Chapter 11

The employer–employee relationship

Staff can be a company's greatest asset. Developing a product range or an innovative range of services, cornering the market, carving new ones or creating market niches and becoming highly profitable are all possible only with the support, skills, and talent of your staff. Good personnel or human resources management is a key component in running a successful company.

Managing employer–employee relations can be difficult. People are not predictable, like production processes. There is no magic formula for inspiring loyalty, or resolving personality conflicts between your staff. However, the art of motivation can be learnt and courses on dealing with conflict, negotiation skills and assertiveness are available, all of which can help to build an effective team. For information contact your local Business Link★ advice unit (see page 15), the Institute of Directors★ or the Industrial Society,★ or look up the DfEE★ web site.

Most successful businesses manage to inspire and keep their staff through a combination of sound working practices, positive interaction between management and employees and a good system of pay, conditions and rewards. This chapter explains how identifying your company's values, improving communication and introducing flexible working can benefit your business. It also shows how to introduce new employees successfully as your business grows.

Communicating with employees

It is advisable to put communication networks in place and set up an incentive and reward system in your business from the start (see page 52). If all your employees feel valued, appreciated and capable of contributing to the running of the company, they will be more likely to accept change of any kind. Bad management practices and a failure to keep staff properly informed can lead to rumours circulating around the workplace. Companies with good communication structures enable employees to express their opinions, and listen to what they say. Staff need to know who they can talk to about new ideas or problems and need assurance that their comments will be communicated to the relevant person. If satisfactory networks are in place, this can enable an organisation to be creative and innovative (see Chapter 4).

Successful companies often have a defined communication structure. For example, employees may be divided into work teams with a team leader. This arrangement is designed to motivate staff, and to encourage:

- quality control (other team members or the team leader may check work)
- creativity (teams may have regular meetings with any ideas being taken to management), and
- problem-solving on a one-to-one basis (team members can ask advice from team leaders).

Everyone should be able to talk to the boss. In very large organisations only the team leader may communicate upwards, although an open-door policy may enable managers and staff to communicate about confidential matters.

Essential information for employees

As well ensuring that communication networks are in place and informing employees about your company's values (see page 160), they need to be supplied with practical information on how the business operates. This is particularly important in the case of new employees, who should be given an induction which enables the provision of key facts. For example, written guidance might cover:

- **basic employee working conditions** The rules on holidays, sick leave, facilities etc.
- **lines of communication** The office hierarchy, team structures, open door policies, suggestion box, staff newsletter and so on. This is more appropriate for larger companies

- **rules that have to be obeyed** Policies on personal phone calls and emails, dress code, unauthorised absences, tea breaks and so on
- **incentive schemes** If you have any, what they are for, how often do you give rewards and what is the purpose of the scheme – e.g. to reward productivity, creativity, innovation?
- **health issues** E.g. flu jabs, company health schemes, gym or shower facilities, perks such as free membership of a local health club
- **social aspects** Where the staff noticeboard is, what clubs exist, information about regular office parties, dinners or sporting events
- **awards** Any the company has won or seeks to win again, with employee co-operation.

Some of this detail, such as basic employee working conditions, will be covered in the contract of employment. You could also draw up a staff manual covering different aspects of your business and make sure everyone has access to it.

Introducing new staff

It has long been recognised by psychologists that small businesses which survive the stresses and strains of starting up can become resistant to change. Often, a small group of people who have worked in a company from the beginning become a close-knit unit with a 'family' mentality.

The introduction of new blood bringing in expertise, ideas and talents is vital for the long-term survival of the business. However, expanding a business may cause discomfort and resistance to change among staff who have been there since the early days. A business may effectively suffer from 'growing pains' and experience stress when new members are added.

Reassuring existing employees

Employing new staff often represents a transition period in the life of a business, and may be accompanied by teething problems.

Jealousies and tensions may arise when new staff are recruited – particularly if those people have special skills or knowledge, are being paid more or are taking on someone else's role. It may not be until a new member has achieved a goal or succeeded with a project (won a contract, installed new technology or developed an overseas market, for example) that the tensions begin to disappear.

Sometimes difficulties can only be eased by the strength and wisdom of the owner/manager. He or she must communicate extremely well with the rest of the workforce in order to avoid rumours, imagined 'slights' and hurt feelings. It can help to communicate and agree common goals, set individual objectives, and arrange regular reviews. Employees should be praised when appropriate and criticised constructively. Consulting widely and stimulating discussion will encourage effective decision-making.

To encourage the acceptance of new members, owner/managers should:

* ensure that everyone in the company is informed about new developments
* ensure that staff understand how every aspect of the company works
* enable employees to contribute creatively to the business process
* offer staff the opportunity to voice doubts or suggestions.

Chapter 4 contains advice on how to ensure a creative and productive working environment.

Interviewing new staff

You should use the interview as an opportunity to explain the role to candidates, determine whether they are capable of doing the job and whether they are interested in the company. The candidates should be given the opportunity to ask questions about how the company operates. Sometimes it is advantageous to let a team member take interviewees on a tour of the work facility and talk to them about the company from the point of view of an employee. This gives candidates the opportunity to speak to potential workmates about the business in an informal capacity before the interview takes place. Each applicant should be treated the same way to ensure that no bias occurs.

Using a recruitment agency

If you decide to use a recruitment agency when employing new staff, you should supply as much information as possible to ensure that it matches your company with suitable candidates – for

---

The office services bureau

This small company in the West Country is owned by two sisters and until recently employed four women and one man. The business offered clerical services – word processing, secretarial services and a job placement agency – to small companies in the area. It was decided that, in order for the business to expand, the computer services side should be enlarged so the company could offer a computer consultancy as well as human resources and accounting services. The firm accordingly employed two computer specialists and an assistant. However, with hindsight the owners realised it would have been better to have transferred an existing employee to be the assistant in the new section. The three new employees kept apart from the others and, due to the pressure of setting up a new department, did not interact with the other employees. This set up resentment amongst the longer-serving staff, who felt that their work was being undervalued. Eventually, an employee who had worked at the company for a while advised the owners that they had a damaging situation on their hands. The tensions were resolved by a series of meetings, which gave all parties the chance to air their views. After clearing up these misunderstandings, the owners decided to pay more attention to developing the older side of the business and involved all employees in job enhancement and forward-planning programmes.

---

example, provide a copy of the job description and any other relevant specifications. Speak to the agency direct and be specific about the sort of qualifications, skills and personal attributes you require. It might be worth asking if a representative would like to visit the premises. When the agency sends through candidates' CVs, review these immediately and if they do not meet your criteria, explain to the agency why they are not up to scratch.

Defining your company's values

It can be beneficial to identify your company's values and write them down. This means building up a general picture of your organisation – including the conditions for employees, rules and restrictions, working styles and social aspects – in order to capture its ethos and atmosphere.

Human Resource specialists recommend having a management discussion first in order to canvass opinion – perhaps including all staff if the company is relatively small. Staff can sometimes put forward surprising perceptions of a company and the exercise should therefore be viewed as an opportunity to gather different views. The checklist below provides some starting points.

You may find that conflicting opinions are expressed about the way the business operates, and that the answers you obtain to the questions above are not clear-cut. It can be normal to encounter some grey areas. Human resources experts suggest that it is best not to have a regimented approach to how to handle every situation, but to alter management style according to need.

Organisations vary and what works for one may not work for another. No business should feel under pressure to convey a caring, sharing image. Business needs will always come first. However, owner/managers might want to do a cost-benefit analysis into the benefits that can be obtained from listening to and supporting employees – such as higher morale, higher job satisfaction, more effective work and higher employee retention.

Your company's values can be conveyed to job candidates to help them identify the atmosphere in the workplace. By being clear about the business environment at the interview stage, you are providing important information to the candidate to help him or her make an informed decision about whether or not he or she will fit in with the company.

Beating skills shortages

A study by the FOCUS Central London Training and Enterprise Council in spring 2000 showed that over two-thirds of the companies surveyed were suffering from a shortage of key skilled workers – notably technical authors, data communication experts and business analysts. At the time of writing, some employers were becoming desperate and had resorted to fast and furious headhunting, in particular targeting IT and e-commerce specialists. According to the Computing Services and Software Association in 2000 there are global shortages of skilled IT workers, which means that competi-

Checklist: Identifying the values of your business

Answering the following questions will help you to 'take the temperature' of your business and chart formally the prevailing approaches and attitudes within it.

- Is your company hierarchical (e.g. departments report to department heads, who report to directors, who report to the Board) or is it team-based (groups of people working on projects, with shared responsibilities)?
- Is there a communication policy and what form does it take? For example, does your company have strictly vertical lines of communication upwards to the Board; a free communication policy (where anyone can talk to anyone else, no matter how high up the managerial scale, about a problem); or a computer-based noticeboard for posting information, etc.?
- Does your company expect employees to be team players or does it encourage individual achievement?
- Are staff encouraged to be creative and/or analytical?
- Are long working hours and a high degree of commitment expected?

tion in this field is particularly fierce. Other sectors are also facing skilled worker shortages – at the time of writing, nursing and many other areas of the health service were particularly affected, and the UK was lacking trained actuaries.

The oil and gas consultancy

This small company, based in Aberdeen, decided to expand the side of its operation that designed and ran safety training courses for oil and gas rig workers. It also produced safety manuals. However, it proved extremely difficult to find the necessary skilled personnel, even though the company was using several recruitment agencies. Eventually the company was forced to employ Canadians and English-speaking specialists from Norway and Russia on short-term contracts in order to fill the skills gap.

- Does your company offer training programmes?
- Is there a policy on flexible working hours or job-sharing?
- Is a quality control system in place?
- Does your company work to targets and do employees get commission?
- Are incentive schemes or rewards for special achievements offered?
- What is your company's policy on maternity leave, staff absence in the event of children's illnesses and employing senior citizens?
- Does your company have any rules about interaction with customers and suppliers (e.g. are first-name terms permissible, while accepting free lunches or holidays is forbidden)?
- How does your company cope with absenteeism?
- Does your company encourage leisure activities for staff?
- Is there a dress and personal appearance code?
- Do your staff have to wear uniforms and do you have an acceptable standard for those uniforms?
- Do your staff have their own desks and are there any rules about personal effects (e.g. plants, photographs etc.)?

The price of desperation

Companies that operate in industries with skill shortages, or require, say, skilled IT personnel to develop a new part of the business, may have to pay a high price for acquiring talent. In high-priced industries, 21-year-old graduates now consider large salaries, share options, big pensions, guaranteed-term contracts and guaranteed partnerships as a normal start-up package. The companies that cannot offer the best packages do not get the best people.

Employing immigrant workers

Because of problems with skills shortages, the government has set up a 'fast-track' immigration procedure for key workers which enables non-European applicants for work permits in certain key jobs to cut the waiting period from three months to just one week in approximately 80 per cent of cases. The scheme is similar to those that operate in Ireland, Germany, the US and Australia.

The scheme came into full force in March 2001 and includes:

- an increase in the length of time a work permit lasts. Fast-track applications can result in a work permit being granted for up to four years, as opposed to one year (the average)
- a facility to allow overseas students studying in the UK to exchange their student visas for work permits without having to return home first and apply from their country of origin
- 'season ticket' permits for key workers who need to work for UK companies for short periods but on a regular basis.

These moves are likely to benefit the many UK consultancies that employ foreign specialists. For more information on employing foreign workers, see *The Which? Guide to Employment*, available from Which? Books.*

Developing your own staff

As the UK switches over to an economy based on service industries instead of manufacturing, the skills shortages seem likely to increase, despite the import of overseas workers. One solution might be a national training programme to generate home-grown talent. However, employers should not ignore the people who work for them. They have an extremely valuable resource in their own staff, and should seek to groom employees and provide them with relevant training. It can be beneficial to identify those with potential and provide assistance with further education where appropriate. This could be linked to a requirement to pay back the money if the employee does not stay with the company within a certain timeframe, to ensure that the owner/manager gets a return on his or her investment.

Flexible working

Many companies have found that flexible working is the best perk that they can offer workers. This might take the form of job sharing or home working, while some businesses have completely flexible start and finish times provided employees work agreed daily hours – for example, some companies allow staff to travel to and from work at off-peak times.

Flexible working can improve job satisfaction and suits staff with children and those who work well outside the office environment.

However, some people find the isolation of working from home daunting and prefer the social interaction of the office or factory. It is important to manage staff successfully from a distance and put effective communication methods in place. The benefits of flexible working for employers are savings on costs and a more productive business. Some economic forecasters believe that adopting flexible working is the only way for companies in the UK to achieve maximum productivity and creativity during the 21st century.

Job sharing and shift work

A job share consists of two people sharing the same role and responsibilities. For example, if a 40-hour working week is shared equally, each employee would work a 20-hour working week. This often occurs where an employee wishes to work only part-time, but the employer needs to have the job covered on a full-time basis. Keeping business open for longer periods than the standard 40-hour working week is made possible by shift working. How this is split would depend on the needs of the business. For a 12-hour day, the split, by mutual agreement, could mean that one employee works from 8a.m. until 2p.m. and the other from 2p.m. until 8p.m. In both cases, employers should keep in mind the need for an effective hand over. This may mean some overlap.

The corporate bank

Two female employees at this bank share a senior management role looking after business customers. The clients are shared equally between them, and each woman follows the activities of her partner closely. They overlap in the office on one day a week and check their phones and email on their days off. The pair agreed to undergo personality testing by the bank, to ensure the partnership represents the best possible 'fit' (management look for similar working styles). Both women describe the job share as resembling a marriage, with flexibility the key to success.

Home working

British Telecom predict that one in four people will work from home by 2025; other sources suggest higher figures. Many large companies have already instituted schemes whereby a high percentage of IT personnel work mainly at home, connected to the office by an intranet system or by email.

Home working allows a certain amount of flexibility, but employees may not be able to fit in the work entirely when it suits them as certain time frames will be dictated by the needs of the business. Core working hours must be agreed to enable accessibility. It is important that employers can trust home workers, since they are not able to see them. Effective communication methods need to be developed and agreed on to prevent workers feeling isolated.

Teleworking

The rise of home working is linked to the growth of the personal computer industry. An increasing number of 'teleworkers' carry out electronic tasks from home while attached to their offices via computer links.

Owner/managers must meet certain health and safety requirements when employing home workers – see 'Setting up a successful system', opposite. Teleworkers should be trained to carry out their work safely, and standards for the display screen, keyboard, lighting and user space should be met. The regulations that affect teleworkers are the Health and Safety at Work Act 1974, the Health and Safety (Display Screen Equipment) Regulations 1992, and the Provision and Use of Work Equipment Regulations 1992.

Other forms of flexible working

Some companies without official home working policies encourage their employees to pursue activities outside the office instead of being desk-based, and reduce their physical capacity accordingly. For example, a company with 4,500 employees might only have office space for 2,500. The rest are out dealing with clients, working from home or networking. When they come into headquarters they park their laptops wherever there is room – there are no personal workspaces. This concept is called hot-desking and is growing in popularity. It can certainly be cost-effective for large companies to consider this option. One large London firm of surveyors estimated that office space in London costs £8,000 per person per year. For advice on keeping overheads down see page 63.

'Road warriors' is the new name that has been coined to describe the army of on-the-road sales staff and other mobile workers who rarely come back to head office but just keep in contact by mobile communications. For example, some lorry drivers never see their head office – they simply respond to fax, email or WAP instructions to pick up and deliver loads. Similarly, British Telecom has 3,500 flexible workers – mostly engineers – based at home, who receive and act upon electronic instructions.

The 24-hour office

Due to technological developments and the globalisation of business relationships, the 24-hour society has become a reality. Some companies, particularly those operating in the field of new technology, maintain a presence around the clock in order to service different time zones around the world. This requires continuous, flexible shifts of employees, working as teams, to cover the tasks in hand – an evolution from the old nine-to-five.

Setting up a successful system

Flexible working involves a great deal of preparatory work. As an employer you are still responsible for that employee, even if he or she is based at home. You must comply with health and safety regulations and should inspect each home workplace, provide training where necessary and ensure that any equipment is safe and regularly tested. When setting up arrangements for staff to work from home, you will need to address the following issues:

- **health and safety concerns** Where is the employee going to work and are the conditions safe? Remember that even the quality of light in the home office area is important. If you are expecting staff to construct items at home, you will have to consider the provision of equipment and training. The Health and Safety Executive★ can advise on working conditions
- **restrictions** Clauses in the employee's mortgage or lease may prohibit conducting business from home. It is the employee's responsibility to inform his or her landlord or mortgage provider of the change of workplace
- **availability and security of parking** This is important if you are expecting the employee to keep a company vehicle such as a lorry or van, possibly with equipment in, outside the house
- **data protection** If the employee is handling sensitive data there could be security issues

- **insurance** Both home and company insurance must fully cover the employee, equipment, third parties and the company from any problems or claims – see page 195. The employer normally insures any equipment provided. Employees may be required to inform their home and contents insurer that extra IT equipment has been provided and that they are working from home. If there is any increase in premiums, the employer should consider picking up the tab
- **special requirements** For example, structural alterations to soundproof, strengthen or fireproof the property.

For more information see *Homeworking (Guidance for Employers and Employees on Health and Safety)*, a publication available from the Health and Safety Executive.

Staying in touch

Flexible working requires a special degree of trust, and clear channels of communication are essential. One drawback of home working is that employees are not visible at a workstation and cannot be supervised directly. Employers need to set clear goals for achievement, and should motivate and reward the employee so that he or she can meet targets and work in a self-sufficient manner.

Job sharers may need to pool essential information between them, which will require people being able to get in touch with the office on their days off. Methods of passing on key details between the job sharers should be devised.

Correct record-keeping is important. For example, engineers going out on repair jobs need some means of telling head office that a job has been done that the customer has verified the task, while their employer needs to be able to communicate changes in job specifications, timings and other requirements. Equipment such as mobile phones and pagers can help the people involved in flexible working arrangements to stay in touch – see Chapter 5.

In order to facilitate communication and combat isolation, there has to be some provision for homeworkers to meet up with each other and their bosses from time to time. This can provide a forum for creative input from workers that may enable a company to keep ahead in the marketplace. People working out in the field are the valuable eyes and ears of a company and can contribute much to policy-making. Periodic get-togethers of regional teams and managers, enabling everyone to compare working problems and discuss relevant issues, can be valuable.

The marketing consultancy

This Hampshire-based company has a staff of 21, all of whom are on flexible-working schedules. The MD bases her working life around the needs of her children. Her co-directors either job-share, are part-time, or fit in around the others. The main body of staff have all agreed among themselves complementary working schedules which allow them to meet the other needs in their lives. The company is always fully covered, productivity is good and the clients' requirements are always put first. The MD regards flexible working as the greatest perk a small business can offer: 'Most people, particularly women with families, regard flexible working as far more important than getting more money at a bigger company. It is also a great motivator. The staff give of their best at all times and they know that they will be covered by someone else if they need the latitude for some problem at home. We have no absenteeism. In fact, we even have women who, if they have to stay at home because their child is ill, will come in and do their work in the evening when their husband is home and can take over the domestic situation.'

Managing absenteeism

Absenteeism is common and can affect the productivity of a business. You should keep on top of absenteeism problems. Not only does it cost a company a great deal of money throughout the working year but it can also cause resentment among diligent staff if they feel that suitable action is not being taken against persistent offenders.

The following approaches can help to prevent absenteeism:

- keep employees motivated so they are unlikely to take time off
- monitor sickness to identify any patterns of concern: e.g. illness on Monday and/or Friday; frequent short periods of sickness; infrequent illnesses of a long duration
- hold return-to-work interviews to identify the reasons for absence

- investigate whether there is anything the company can do to prevent absence.

If there is an underlying illness problem, you have the right to insist that medical help is sought. Employees should have a section in their contracts of employment stipulating that the company reserves the right to ask any employee to be medically examined by a doctor of the company's choice. Some employers might consider contributing towards medical costs if the employee is valuable and normally contributes a great deal towards the running of the company.

If domestic or personal problems are the cause of absenteeism, these may be solved by introducing flexible working, which has been shown to have a high success rate in reducing absenteeism. This might mean helping the employee to sort out crèche arrangements or giving him or her time off on reduced pay to sort out any immediate difficulties.

Disciplining employees

The circumstances behind absence should be fully investigated and employees should receive a series of verbal and written warnings before dismissal is considered. Disciplinary procedures should be formalised and made available to all employees. Make an attempt to deal with issues informally and to find out what lies behind the attitude before going down the official route. A thorough, unbiased investigation must be carried out to identify whether the situation is serious enough to be dealt with by disciplinary procedures, and the employee has the right to be accompanied by a fellow worker or trade union representative at all times. He or she should also be provided with the opportunity to put across his or her case and any mitigating circumstances. Record-keeping will identify the severity and scale of any problems.

The next chapter investigates the legislation that governs the employer–employee relationship.

Chapter 12

Keeping abreast of legislation

Much of your relationship with your employees is dictated by legislation. The amount of government regulations continues to grow, and existing laws change regularly. It is therefore important to keep up with developments.

The UK is governed by both UK and EU legislation. The purpose of much of this bureaucracy is to bring the UK in line with the rest of Europe and to encourage better working practices and investment in the UK, which in turn will stimulate competition. Some changes have been focused towards improving the work–life balance. The outcome of this should be more motivated employees and increased productivity. However, concerns have been raised about the effect of dealing with bureacracy on small businesses (see below). The possible impact of legislative changes is highlighted in the media, and interested parties, including employers, are invited to comment on the proposals outlined in Green Papers issued by the government.

This chapter looks at how the most recent developments are likely to affect businesses. For full information on employers' statutory obligations, see *The Which? Guide to Employment*. The organisations listed on pages 184–5 can also help.

The burden of red tape

Dealing with legislation can cost employers time and money. The Federation of Small Businesses has stated that government regulations are stifling small firms before they have a chance to grow. The box overleaf highlights the effect of having to administer regulations on SMEs, while ways of relieving the burden are described on pages 185–6.

The cost of legislation

- In 1999 the government dealt out 3,468 new regulations to businesses at a total estimated cost of £30 billion a year.
- In 2001 the Institute of Chartered Surveyors (ICS) criticised the fact that employers are obliged to calculate the amount of working families tax credit in employees' wage packets – in effect acting as unpaid social security agents.
- The ICS asserted that the annual cost of dealing with bureacracy almost doubled in 2000. Firms with up to 50 staff saw the cost of administering laws and regulations rise from £4,700 to £8,000, while for those with fewer than ten employees it rose from £1,700 to £3,600.
- The DTI estimates that enforcing Working Time Regulations costs businesses £2.3bn a year while parental rights leave costs about £35m in lost productivity and engaging temporary staff.
- According to a NatWest Small Business Research Trust survey published in September 2000, the average small business with 10–14 employees spends 31.8 hours a month complying with government regulations and paperwork.

New legislation

This section summarises the latest employment legislation and proposed changes at the time of going to press (April 2001). It does not provide full details of every statute but covers the key points that affect SMEs.

Maternity leave and parental leave

Maternity leave and parental leave are covered by the provisions of the Employment Relations Act 1999, which are due to come into force over 18 months from July 1999.

Maternity leave

Pregnant employees now have the following rights:

- an entitlement to ordinary maternity leave (18 weeks)
- an entitlement to additional maternity leave (29 weeks) for women who have worked for their employer for over a year

- the right to return to work is taken as automatic. A woman no longer has to state that she is exercising her right to return to work.

It has become difficult for employers who have to rely on temporary staff to provide maternity leave cover to maintain a sense of continuity in their companies. Many companies have tried to develop a positive strategy whereby women who are intending to start families are offered the opportunity to job share before, during and after pregnancy.

This can work on several levels. First, it allows the employee to become used to part-time working before the birth and enables her to return easily to part-time work, which is the choice of most returning mothers. Second, it allows the employer to more easily replace the woman on maternity leave with a temp because there is another job sharer already in place to help him or her grasp the job more quickly. Third, job sharing allows the work of the absent employee to be more easily shared amongst others, thereby making the need for additional staff unecessary.

Parental leave

Since 1999 employees whose children were born after 15 December 1999 have had the statutory right to take 13 weeks' unpaid parental leave (this means the father/partner as well as the birth mother). The Prime Minister announced in February 2001 that the government had agreed, in principle, to the introduction of paid paternity leave and also to the introduction from 2003 of paid leave for adoptive parents. The government is looking into how to give extra help to disabled mothers or those who work irregular hours, such as nurses.

A study of 33 large organisations undertaken in 2000 by Incomes and Data Services (IDS) found that no organisations were offering paid parental leave. However, many made enhanced maternity leave and pay packages available. Just under half of the companies surveyed opted to enhance the statutory entitlements of 18 or 40 weeks' maternity leave, with the most common maximum duration being one year. Most of the organisations offered employees better-than-statutory payments, with many providing full pay for all or part of the 18-week statutory maternity pay period.

Green Paper on work and parents

At the time of writing, the government was seeking feedback on its Green Paper entitled 'Work and Parents: Competitiveness and Choice'. In this document the government proposes to:

- support parents around the time of a child's birth
- extend the unpaid maternity leave period to one year
- allow both mother and father to share this period of unpaid maternity leave
- increase the flat rate of maternity pay
- extend the maternity pay period from 18 weeks to 26 weeks
- introduce a right to paid parental leave for adopters
- give fathers a short period of paid paternity leave on the same rate as maternity pay
- support parents in the workplace
- increase parental leave for parents of disabled children
- allow working parents the right to time off for the primary healthcare needs of their children
- allow women to return to their jobs after maternity leave and work reduced hours
- possibly allow both parents the right to work reduced hours after maternity leave ends
- possibly allow fathers to work reduced hours while the maternity leave period is in progress.

The government also encouraged debate on whether the legislation on maternity leave and pay should be simplified; whether more SMEs should be able to obtain complete repayment of the money paid out on Statutory Maternity Pay (and perhaps a small amount of compensation); and whether Statutory Maternity Pay should be paid direct to mothers (2010 was suggested as a target date).

Comments were also invited on the following proposed measures:

- the right for employers to refuse a request to work reduced hours, if they can show that it would cause harm to the business (businesses were asked to help define the yardstick by which 'harm' is measured)
- exemptions from requests to work reduced hours for businesses with fewer than a certain number of employees

- the introduction of a standards system – like kitemarking – to be awarded to companies that offer flexible working opportunities
- the reimbursement of small businesses which adopt flexible working.

The Green Paper also made reference to ways in which the government might improve its two-way communications with businesses – through an easily accessible Internet Flexible Gateway, backed up by a call centre, for example. (Chapter 5 looks in more detail at the growing area of business-to-administration e-commerce.)

The thinking behind the Green Paper is that employers might be more receptive to flexible working if they were given financial incentives to adopt such strategies – rather like farmers being given subsidies to grow certain crops. However, as most business people know, human resources is not quite as straightforward as farming. Many people do not want to work flexible hours, nor do they want to job share or work shifts. Small businesses, in particular, can find flexible working a difficult strategy to implement. The fewer people a company has, the less adaptable it is. During the consultation period, the government is leaving the door open for businesses to put forward special cases explaining why they should be exempt from any kind of flexible working.

Working Time Regulations

The Working Time Regulations (1998) provide the following basic rights and protections for adult employees:

- workers cannot be required to work more than an average limit of 48 hours per week over a 17-week reference period (though they can choose to work more if they want to)
- nightworkers cannot be required to work more than an average limit of 8 hours in 24 hours
- a right for nightworkers to receive free health assessment
- a right to 11 hours' rest a day
- a right to one day off a week
- a right to an in-work rest break if the working day is longer than six hours
- a right to four weeks' paid leave a year.

Employers will need to record the working hours of employees if staff who are contracted to work less than 48 hours per week exceed that amount over a 17-week reference period. Overtime records must be sent to the Health and Safety Executive (HSE).*

Young Workers' Directive

The government implemented the remaining provisions of the Young Workers' Directive into UK law between December 2000 and March 2001. These relate to the working time of adolescent workers (young people above the minimum school-leaving age of 16 but below the age of 18).

It is proposed that three aspects of the directive will be amended to deal with young workers:

- **Working time** The Directive limits young workers' working time to 8 hours a day and 40 hours a week. There is no provision for averaging working time over a reference period, nor can individuals opt out. However, the limits on working time may be excluded where there are objective grounds – for example: operational or customer requirements in the sector or occupation concerned (such as the need for supermarkets to restock shelves at night when the stores are closed and deliveries are made); the need for continuity of service or production; or foreseeable surges of activity (such as seasonal work).
- **Night work between midnight and 4am** Work by young workers is prohibited during this period. However, the Directive allows exemptions for employment in the armed forces and the police; employment in hospitals or similar establishments; employment in connection with cultural, artistic, sporting or advertising activities; and employment in shipping or fisheries.
- **Night work between 10pm and 6am or between 11pm and 7am** Work by young workers is prohibited during one or other of these periods. Exemptions are as above, with the addition of employment in agriculture, hotels and catering, retailing, postal services and newspaper deliveries. A requirement is in place for young workers to be adequately supervised during these hours where it is necessary for their protection.

The government also expressed some concern in its consultation document over the issue of young workers' safety when travelling to and from work at night, and recommended that employers be sensitive to the demands placed upon young workers during examination periods.

Enforcement of the regulations is split between two bodies. The statutory entitlements (e.g. the rest periods and breaks and paid annual leave) are enforced through employment tribunals, although the Advisory Conciliation and Arbitration Service (ACAS)★ will initially endeavour to resolve any dispute. The working time limits are enforced by the HSE and local authorities.

The Employment Relations Act 1999

Most of the provisions of this Act came into force in 2000 and covered the following points:

- **Trade union recognition and derecognition** Employers must recognise an independent trade union in a company employing 21 or more workers if it is the wish of the majority of the workforce. The Central Arbitration Committee (CAC) will decide whether the union should be recognised and select the appropriate bargaining unit in the event of a dispute. It will also, if necessary, impose a legally binding procedure for bargaining about pay, working hours and holidays. The Act also provides for changes in the bargaining unit and for the derecognition of unions, and protects workers against detriment or dismissal for exercising their rights under the schedule.
- **Ballots and notices** The Act removes the requirement for unions to disclose to employers the names of members whom they are balloting or calling on to take industrial action. It enables a union to extend the validity of its industrial action ballot by a maximum of a further four weeks if both the union and employer agree. It provides greater scope for the courts to disregard small accidental failures in the organisation of industrial ballots and it clarifies the circumstances in which a union can hold aggregate industrial action ballots of members in separate workplaces.
- **Right to be accompanied** This provides workers with the right to be accompanied by a fellow worker or trade union offi-

cial to any disciplinary or grievance hearing. This excludes any members of the security and intelligence services and only applies to hearings which are serious in nature and could result in a formal warning or other action against the worker.

- **Other rights of individuals** These concern: the unfair dismissal of striking workers; the unfair dismissal of workers who refuse to accept a contract which differs from a collective agreement; preventing employees on fixed-term contracts from waiving their right to claim unfair dismissal at the end of their term; ensuring that part-time workers have the same rights as full-time workers; and exempting religious communities from adhering to the national minimum wage.
- **Partnerships at work** This authorises the Secretary of State to make funding available to promote partnerships at work. This fund is being developed as a mechanism to provide support for training managers and employee representatives to help them work together, negotiate better and form working partnerships.
- **Employment agencies** Measures have been proposed to reform the working practices of employment agencies so that they do not abuse or monopolise the services of workers who register with them.
- **Unfair dismissal awards** These provisions simplified the existing system of additional and special awards and linked the limits on various payments and employment tribunal awards to changes in the Retail Prices Index. The maximum limit for unfair dismissal compensatory awards was increased to £50,000. There have been indexations since October 1999. It also removed any limit on awards in certain cases (e.g. health and safety problems). Another statute that came into force in 1999 (although not part of the Act) was the reduction of the length of service qualification for unfair dismissal from two years to one.

The changes in the length of service qualifications and the raising of maximum limits of awards (or in some cases, removals of limits) is likely to make little practical difference to employers provided they have not been negligent or dismissed anyone unfairly. However, guilty employers face greater financial penalties, and the changes are likely to create a burden on the tribunals, since more people are now allowed to bring a grievance before them.

Telecommunications (Lawful Business Practice) (Interception of Communications) Regulations

These regulations state that after an employer has made reasonable efforts to inform staff that communications through the firm's computers may be monitored, the firm is entitled to read employees' emails and monitor web site access for the purpose of identifying unlawful or improper use of its communications systems. The regulations, described as a 'snoopers' charter', have already had a powerful effect on businesses and resulted in high-profile sackings.

Many companies have formulated written policies concerning email and Internet use. This makes life easier for employers and employees because a written code leaves no room for doubt as to what constitutes misuse. In a study undertaken in January 2000, Incomes Data Services (IDS) found that the following provisions featured most often in codes:

- use of communications for personal means is either forbidden or limited
- confidential information must be encrypted before being sent via email
- disclaimers and signature files must be attached to emails sent to external parties
- employees must follow general housekeeping good practices (e.g. the regular deletion of emails)
- employees are advised to use appropriate etiquette when sending emails (e.g. using upper case is considered to be the equivalent of SHOUTING)
- inappropriate messages are banned, including those which constitute sexual harassment or are offensive on the grounds of race, religion or gender
- employees must not send potentially defamatory email messages criticising other individuals or organisations
- employees must not access or download inappropriate material, such as pornography, from the Internet
- employees must be aware of copyright concerns when downloading or forwarding material to others
- employees must ensure the accuracy of any information posted on a corporate web site and update it regularly.

Infringements of email regulations

- Fifteen traders and staff were fired in 2000 by City bank Merrill Lynch for circulating pornography on the bank's internal email system.
- The TUC produced figures to show that many UK workers were abusing the firm's computer systems. The weekly cost of workers accessing the web site of the TV programme *Big Brother* was said to have hit a total of £1.41 million at the show's peak of popularity.
- The editor of *The Sun* sacked one of his senior columnists when he discovered that she was trading information and insults about her boss, and e-flirting with the editor of the rival newspaper *The Mirror*. Press reports suggested she had been engaged in a four-month correspondence with this rival editor which amounted to nearly 5,000 emails.

The Data Protection Act

The Data Protection Act was introduced to protect the rights of individuals by preventing the misuse of data stored in computers and ensuring that the data is accurate and secure. Many SMEs are still uncertain as to how it affects them – yet the implications for small businesses are far-reaching. Any business that has started a new data collection process since March 2000 must comply with the law, although existing data networks are not required to be fully compliant until October 2001. New web sites must be compliant from the moment they are set up.

The Act gives individuals the right to know what data is held on them, the right to correct or erase that data, and the right to compensation if that data causes harm through inaccuracy, loss or misuse. Companies that store and process personal data must place their names on a central register, which is made available to the public.

Any company gathering personal data (for example, a company conducting market research in the street) should give participating individuals full information on how that data will be used, and should obtain signed agreement from those individuals to permit the use of that data.

The increased use of intranet systems and the Internet has meant that electronic data may pass between several companies. Under the provisions of the Act, businesses are responsible not only for the security of data on their own systems, but also for data on the systems of companies that are in partnership with them – such as suppliers, customers, outsourced human resources administrators and credit-checking companies. It can be difficult to decide what is your company's responsibility and what isn't. The SBS★ web site offers advice.

Improving data protection

The Data Protection Act is difficult to police, as evidenced by the breaches in security common amongst Internet traders (see page 86). You should ensure that your company has a good security system to protect yourself against fraud. For maximum effectiveness, get an expert to design a system that everyone understands and can operate.

Security specialists recommend conducting an information audit so that you know where all data goes and is stored, and to whom it is transmitted. It is advisable to separate out different information processes – for example, personnel records from customer information – as this makes it easier to develop a tailored security system for each one. Train all your staff, including the boardroom, in data protection measures, and take regular back-ups.

The British Standards Institute (BSI)★ suggests a framework on how to initiate, implement and maintain information security within an organisation. There are three stages:

1) Create a management framework for information which sets the direction, aims and objectives of information security and defines a policy which can be implemented with management support.
2) Assess your security risks. Spending on controls should be balanced against the value of the information and other assets at risk, and the business implications of those risks.
3) Put controls in place so that the identified security risks are reduced to an acceptable level (this will vary from company to company).

For more information, see *British Standard on Information Security Management BS7799* which can be purchased from the BSI.

Many employees now receive and transmit information from outside the central workplace due to the increase in flexible working and homeworking (see Chapter 11). A survey conducted in 2000 by MORI of 2,000 mobile computer users found that 60 per cent of them did not use a password and 75 per cent did not put security measures in place to protect electronic information when they were out of the office. Most computer systems have security procedures built in, but people are lax about using them. Refresher training can help to emphasise their importance.

Stakeholder pensions

At the time of writing, over 75 per cent of small businesses in the UK do not provide pensions for their staff. The introduction of stakeholder pensions in October 2001 is an attempt to improve the options for employees.

Stakeholder pensions are low-cost pensions meant for people who currently do not have appropriate pension options available to save for their retirement. A stakeholder scheme is a trust or a similar arrangement, and works the same way as most existing employers' pension schemes. A scheme must meet certain requirements, such as limits on costs and the provision of information to members, and be registered with the Occupational Pensions Regulatory Authority (OPRA).★ Stakeholder pensions could be a good option for employees who earn more than £10,000 a year. If people earn less than that it may be better for them to stay in the state pension scheme.

Unless your company is exempt (see below), you must arrange access to a stakeholder pension scheme for all employees who earn more than the NI lower earnings limit (currently £76 per week). The final decision to take up the scheme rests with the employees.

Choosing and setting up a stakeholder pension are covered in detail in *Stakeholder pensions – a guide for employers*, which is available from DSS Publications★ and can be downloaded from *www.dss.gov.uk/publications/dss/2000/stakeholder_emp/*

Your business is exempt if:

- you employ fewer than five people (you must include all your employees)
- you already offer an occupational pension scheme that all your staff can join within a year of working for you

- you offer your staff access to a personal pension scheme which meets the following conditions:
  i. it is available to all employees who should have access to a stakeholder pension scheme
  ii. you contribute an amount equal to at least 3 per cent of the employee's basic pay to the personal pension
  iii. the scheme has no penalties for members who stop contributing or who transfer their pension
  iv. you deduct the employee's contributions from his or her pay and send them to the personal pension provider if the employee asks you
- you offer an occupational scheme for some staff and a personal pension scheme for the others, and the schemes meet with the conditions above.

You do not have to provide access to a stakeholder pension scheme for any employee:

- who has worked for you for less than three months in a row
- who is a member of your occupational pension scheme
- who cannot join your existing pension scheme because he or she is under 18 years of age or within five years of the scheme's normal pension age
- who could have joined your existing scheme but decided not to
- whose earnings have not reached the National Insurance lower earnings limit for at least three months in a row
- who cannot join a stakeholder scheme because of Inland Revenue restrictions (e.g. the employee does not normally reside in the UK).

Note the following important points:

- If you take on your fifth employee after 8 July 2001, you will have only three months from when he/she joins to go through the selection process and designate a stakeholder pension scheme.
- Companies with five or more employees could be fined as much as £50,000 if they do not make provision for their staff by October 2001. This is the maximum penalty for non-compliance. However, OPRA has stated that it is unlikely to impose

fines on employers as long as they can show that they are in the process of putting a scheme in place.

- Other penalties will be incurred if: you do not set up a record of the payments you make; you do not keep the record up to date; you do not send the record to the scheme provider; you do not tell the provider about any changes; and you do not make the correct payments on time.

According to research conducted by Scottish Amicable in 2000, four out of five small businesses were unlikely to meet the October 2001 deadline for putting a scheme in place. More than half of those surveyed had never heard of stakeholder pensions and did not know that they were legally obliged to provide them for employees. Axa concurs with these findings. In research carried out in 2000, the organisation found that 67 per cent of businesses with five or more employees had not read the DSS guide that was mailed to them explaining stakeholder pensions. It is important that your business is fully informed about the scheme and capable of offering employees the best deal.

Help with legislation

It is crucial for owner/managers to keep up with the regulations. The following sources can provide information on the latest developments and offer guidance on aspects of employment law.

Ways of keeping informed

Useful publications include *Tolley's Company Secretary Handbook* and titles from Croner and the Stationery Office.★ The Stationery Office can supply copies of legislation documents and the SBS★ provides excellent employment law advice.

Technology offers a solution in the form of the many web sites that give instant updates on all regulations and legislation. The most significant development is the government's own web sites, the most useful of which are listed here.

The government site *www.open.gov.uk/cctagis.whatsnew* provides daily updates on the latest information from various government departments. The site contains one month's worth of information, and has useful links. Another helpful and user-friendly site is Direct Access Government at *www.dag-business.gov.uk*. Developed by the SBS to help businesses cut through red tape, it allows surfers to access regulatory information and print out relevant forms. A 'what's new' section displays every piece of legislation to have come out that month – this might include everything from regulations pertaining to catteries, to health and safety legislation. You can also register the areas of regulation that you are interested in and receive daily emailed links to the latest document releases. The DTI employment site at *www.dti.gov.uk/er/links* has a 'Useful Links' page which enables you to access the sites of 82 organisations including government bodies, business advice sites, business publishers and regulatory bodies, plus overseas sites (e.g. the EU and the US government).

In addition to government sources there is a vast range of companies and commercial services which offer advice online. Some merely offer sales spiel but there are many good sites. *www.clearlybusiness.com*, a web site backed by Barclays and Freeserve, has teamed up with the Prince's Youth Business Trust to create a programme aimed at improving the experience of using the Internet among small businesses. The Sunday Times Enterprise Network claims that it 'provides fast-track solutions to business challenges'. The Economist Intelligence Unit has launched a free e-business forum for senior executives which has a wealth of business information experience behind it, and can be found at *www.ebusinessforum.com*. The web site of employment law consultancy EmpLaw at *www.Emplaw.co.uk* has a regularly updated 'what's new' section.

Easing the administrative burden

As already mentioned, keeping up with regulations can be time-consuming. Services exist which can help businesses to adminster legislation and deal with paperwork.

One option might be to outsource human resources (HR). If HR administrative matters are dealt with externally, this frees owner/managers from having to wade through the compulsory paperwork. Although the practice is mostly restricted to large organisations, the Chartered Institute of Personnel and

Development reports that more HR service companies are developing systems for small clients. An IDS study in December 2000 entitled *Outsourcing HR Administration* examined arrangements in nine organisations among which some smaller companies were included.

The property development company

A small property development company which specialises in buying up and refurbishing old houses recently outsourced all its HR administration to an HR services company. This involved the property company being linked up to the service company's intranet system. Personnel information from the property company was then fed into the system.

The system works in the following way. The service company administers the payroll each month, works out benefits and tax and deals with all the necessary administrative tasks and transactions. All the property company has to do is formulate policy issues (e.g. relationships with trade unions, pay negotiations, holidays and conditions). For the property company, the arrangement has removed all the worry of paperwork, calculations, form-filling and ensuring compliance with regulations. The MD claims that the new system is of particular benefit since staff are on a variety of contracts, which used to be 'quite a headache' to administer before they were taken over.

Technology can also help. A small but growing number of companies provide high-speed Internet access combined with online accountancy, payroll and stock control and data back-up services. Smaller companies using these services can remain permanently connected to the Internet at a fixed cost without needing to log on and off each time.

The red tape will never go away, but it is now possible to be better informed and to buy in services that will help you deal with employment regulations. The next chapter deals with planning for the unexpected.

Chapter 13

Contingency planning

Sometimes called 'business continuity', 'disaster recovery' or 'emergency planning', contingency planning involves preparing for your company's worst-case scenario. You should not put this off – it needs to be done *now*.

What is an emergency to your company? It is any event which effectively stops you doing business, even just for half a day, or threatens the continuity of your business. Events that might cause difficulties include:

- **natural disasters** e.g. flooding, mudslides, earthquakes, impassable snow, hurricanes
- **personnel problems** e.g. 'flu epidemics, transport strikes, sabotage by a disgruntled employee
- **utilities failure** e.g. loss of power, water or telecommunications
- **computer problems** e.g. loss of data, viruses, bad programming and so on.

The possibilities are endless. For example, a major supplier goes bust overnight. Your biggest customer breaks contract. An employee sells company information to rivals. Your company causes an environmental disaster by leakage of chemicals into the water supply or by a lorry driver illegally dumping toxic waste in an unauthorised place . . .

All sorts of things can happen to companies – so why don't most companies plan for the worst? The truth is that most SMEs would rather not think about it and prefer to conduct their business on a 'fingers crossed' basis.

Regrettably, one disadvantage of a techology driven business world is that disasters can crop up with monotonous regularity (see box overleaf).

Businesses caught out by the unexpected

- A large insurance company 'lost' over £270,000 in premium payments in a single day because a virus infected the electronic data interchange system between it and its bank. It took them six weeks to remedy the situation, during which time the company paid huge amounts of overtime to staff who had to recover the data manually.
- A medium-sized doctor's practice in Yorkshire lost its entire pharmacy database, including patient information, when a system crash caused it to discover that it had been incorrectly saving data on supposed back-up files. It was unable to recover the information.
- A cinema chain lost over one week's worth of business in five regional cinemas when its computerised telephone booking service went wrong and cut people off in mid-sentence. The problem was not discovered for two days because the company had not published an administration number anywhere – so customers could not report the fault.
- A bank in Kent was put out of business for nearly three weeks due to severe flooding. No one, including the staff, could get to the bank and even if anyone had gained access the equipment was ruined. There was an 'off-site recovery plan', but unfortunately all the back-up files were stored in the flooded bank.
- A small food manufacturing company lost two days of business because two very large trees were brought down across the road during a severe storm, which blocked access to and from the factory for the delivery lorries. It took council workers a day and a half to cut up the trees with chainsaws.

Risk assessment and business impact analysis

Risk assessment and business impact analysis are part of the initial analysis that you have to make before formulating a contingency plan. It is necessary to look in detail at your company's vulnerabilities and weaknesses. These are not the same thing: a vulnerability is an area which could expose you to threat from outside influences; a weakness is something within your company that needs to be strengthened. For example, making a large part of your business dependent upon one big customer is vulnerability with a capital V. If that customer goes to the wall, you go with him or her. A weakness might consist of having shoddy quality control procedures. For example, if you make toys and one of those toys comes apart and injures a small child because of your failure to evaluate critically the manufacturing process, the resultant bad publicity could lead to a drop in sales. These are extreme examples, but both represent disasters. It is crucial to examine all the possible areas of risk. Once you have identified the vulnerabilities and weaknesses of your company, you can insure against likely mishaps (see page 195).

You can do something about some areas of risk by taking what professional contingency planners call 'risk reduction measures'. This means minimising the risks that you can identify and planning for the disasters that you may not be able to avoid. In order to identify how you can reduce risk you have to sit down with your managers and conduct a business impact analysis to assess how a particular scenario might affect your company. For example, what would be the impact on your business if you were without electrical power for 16 hours? Would you have to shut down completely? Do you have another site that you could transfer to? Do you have a back-up generator?

Once you have been able to work through what would happen if any type of disaster occurred, then it is time to draw up a contingency plan. You need to put down in writing the procedures for all staff to follow in the event of flooding/hurricanes/flu epidemics/war – whatever eventualities you can think of.

You also need to work out recovery timings, channels of communication and responsibilities. If you run a business that might attract media attention were it to suffer a setback (some kind of public service, for example), you need to decide who will have the job of speaking to the media, dealing with the public and gathering information (see page 191).

It is a good idea to publish all the information that relates to dealing with disasters in a contingency planning manual (see below), which should be accessible to all staff.

Proposed contents of a contingency planning manual
- The emergency response structure (who does what, who reports to whom).
- Checklists for tasks to be undertaken (e.g. checking parts of a production line or going through records to find whether any errors were present prior to an incident).
- An explanation of emergency procedures (where people are to assemble, where the business will be relocated on a temporary basis).
- Details of the times and locations that are important to reporting systems (where and when designated employees should supply signatures or verbal assurance when checking in).
- Contact numbers (for the regular off-site workforce, or for designated staff in the event of an incident happening overnight).
- Instructions regarding who is allowed to speak to the media, general public, customers or family members, and at what stage.
- Instructions regarding the involvement of the emergency services (covering who is to liaise with them and what they need to be told. For example, if you run a business which uses hazardous chemicals someone would need to advise the Fire Service of any dangers in the event of a fire).
- The names and contact details of designated first-aiders (trained members of staff should be allocated responsibility for sections of the workforce).
- The names and contact details of designated specialists (people who will be on call, day or night, if there is a computer systems failure, machinery breakdown, chemical spillage, etc.)
- A rota detailing the availability of key individuals.
- Up-to-date building plans showing the location of all fire doors, fire-fighting equipment, first-aid equipment, hazardous material storage, and so on.

Teamwork is important

It helps to set up an emergency response team. These are members of staff designated to tackle specific jobs when an emergency occurs.

Your company may be quite small, in which case it is likely to be a case of 'all hands to the pump'. But it still saves time and duplication of effort if everyone is allocated a job before a disaster actually happens. This can also enable certain contingency plans to be put into action. You may decide, for example, that all back-up data should be securely stored (preferably in fireproof cabinets) in the homes of two managers who live in different areas. If you have more than one site, you could consider making arrangements for business activities to be transferred to an another company base in the event of power cuts, flooding or another disaster affecting the main office.

You should establish lines of communication. It can help to break your staff down into smallish cells of people, each of whom report to a leader, who then reports to the person with overall responsibility. For example, if your factory was damaged by a gas explosion, your cell leaders would know that they were responsible for, say, three other people and would concentrate on locating and accounting for those personnel.

A similar principle applies to the allocation of tasks. For example, in the event of a power failure you could decide that one group of people has the task of discovering whether anyone is trapped in lifts in the building, while another group is responsible for making sure that all lighting and heating are turned off at the mains, in case the power comes back on while the building is empty.

Suggestions on what to include in the contingency planning manual are outlined below.

Dealing with the media and the public

Most businesses try to actively court the media, even if just the local press, in order to generate some positive PR. Any company, no matter how small, can find itself the target of unwanted media and public attention in the event of a disaster. (The box below outlines the type of situations that will generate interest.) It therefore pays to be prepared for media interest if you are facing a crisis, particularly if it is a disaster that affects the general public.

If you have identified a vulnerability that could give rise to an incident which would affect people outside the office, you should set up a media response team and a public response team to work alongside each other, and explain the arrangement in your contingency plan.

Let's deal with the media first. It can help if you have already established good relationships with the press, and preferably individual journalists, because you can use these contacts to disseminate the 'right' information in a time of crisis. Adopt an open, honest and positive approach when giving out information. This avoids unnecessary damage to the company's image, is least likely to antagonise the media (if this happens, they may turn to unofficial sources for information which could be inaccurate), and avoids unnecessary distress to the public or friends and relatives of employees affected by the problem.

It is important that the media response team consists of staff who have been trained in responding to pressure from the media and the public in times of emergency. These personnel will be responsible for the controlled release of information and they will be the first point of contact for those calling the company.

As part of your contingency plan, you should put together a fact pack giving background information about your company (its personnel, past activities, health and safety and environmental records, plus any appropriate facts and figures) and update this regularly. This can be used by the media response team to provide journalists with background material. Many companies now post this sort of detail on their web sites, which allows the press to easily access useful information in a time of crisis.

It is vital that the media response team has a separate phone line (even if it only consists of one person), and that the switchboard or system is programmed to divert all media calls to that number. Only the designated media response team members should be allowed to speak to the media, unless the owner/manager decides to make him- or herself available for comment. The team should be trained to give out, in a helpful and friendly manner, *only* the information they are authorised to pass on. They should not be drawn into making personal observations or suggestions. They should not be provoked into emotional responses or speculation on unfolding events, and certainly should not allow themselves to be coaxed into revealing aspects of company policy or discussing issues of liability or compensation.

If a major disaster occurs that attracts a lot of media attention, this could put the team under a lot of pressure and call for back-up. For example, someone might need to liaise between the team and those personnel releasing information, in order to keep the team updated about key facts the and company's latest stance. The team might also need to be told if any sections of the media were becoming more aggressive or, say, hogging the phone lines in pursuit of a story. Incoming calls should be logged so that the company has a record of telephone conversations and times.

The public response team deals with the general public, including relatives and friends of company employees. Their job can be more demanding than that of the media response team, since in the event of a life- or health-threatening emergency they may have to deal with worried, frightened, or even hysterical people concerned about those involved in the incident.

Emergency situations likely to hit the headlines
- A significant unplanned event (i.e. something that will have a major impact on your company), such as: fire; major theft; vandalism; environmental contamination; loss of public data; major failure or loss of control of normal operating systems; computer systems failure; death or injury of an employee on duty; kidnapping of an employee; a bomb threat.
- Threat(s) to:
  a) people (the public, customers)
  b) the environment
  c) property/assets
  d) the image/brand/reputation of the company
  e) the social responsibility of the company.
- Perception of negligence on the part of the company.
- An incident that creates, or is created by, media interest.
- An incident involving external agencies such as the police or the fire brigade.
- An incident with the potential for escalation.

Non-operational emergency situations
- Financial difficulties
- Loss of key personnel
- Hostile takeover
- Partners/shareholders losing confidence in the company.

A public helpline number should be set up and kept separate from the rest of the telephone system. The team should be trained to be sensitive and positive. They need to be able to deal with a range of emotions – from tears to anger – in the people who phone in. They should be trained to give out only authorised information and, even if they know that there has been a bereavement, must never reveal this over the telephone. Systems should be in place to ensure that news of any hospitalisations or fatalities is communicated to relatives face-to-face by the police.

The public response team will need good communications back-up, not only to bring them up-to-date information but also to provide some means of contacting the emergency services if a caller requires additional assistance. For example, an employee injured in a disaster may have a heavily pregnant wife who hears of the accident while on her own and then contacts the company in a distressed state. The team could get the co-ordinator to organise the police or medical services to take supportive action while she speaks to helpline staff.

Emergency drills

Whether or not your company's contingency planning includes media and public response facilities, it is important to keep staff informed on emergency procedures and involve them in regular drills (the same way as you have regular fire drills). These will help to keep employees aware of how to react quickly in all kinds of emergency situations.

Contingency planning experts remark that 'real' disasters are unlikely to unfold in the same way as scenarios you have tested. Your precautions should therefore include action plans for all eventualities, no matter how far-fetched. Be as flexible as possible, and keep procedures up to date. Refresh everyone's memory now and then, particularly if there have been equipment or facility changes.

Do not be like the furniture storage company that forgot to amend its warehouse plans when the facility's internal layout changed. It cost the business dear when it had a major fire outbreak and the fire service found that the building plans were out-of-date and useless.

Loss mitigation

After an emergency it is time to take stock and get out the insurance policies. It is important to ensure that these are up to date and will cover all your losses.

It is not possible to insure against all the risks to which a company may be exposed. But you can insure against most of them. Risk analysis will help you to spot where you are likely to need cover. By identifying your company's vulnerabilities and weaknesses, described earlier, you may be able to eliminate some of the risks. This might be accomplished by changing company strategy or procedures, or by recruitment and training. For example, a company with persistent theft problems could eliminate them by hiring security staff.

The risks that cannot be changed must be insured against wherever possible.

Insuring against risk

The following list details insurance that you are obliged to have, and insurance that you might find useful.

- **Employer's liability** (essential) In January 1999 the government raised the statutory minimum level of cover from £2m to £5m.
- **Replacement of assets** (essential) Full cover for total loss of assets is vital.
- **Consequent loss of business/business interruption** (essential) Full cover is crucial. The indemnity period should be long enough to allow a company to get up and running to its pre-loss trading position.
- **Public liability and third-party liability** (Strongly advised) Cover against accident or harm caused to members of the public by your company or premises, and cover against liability to third parties who are not employees but may be sub-contractors or temps.
- **Environmental impairment liability** Essential if you are involved in any manufacturing process that produces toxic waste or chemical by-products. The insurance company will undertake an environmental audit to ensure that all necessary measures are

in place to contain waste and that your disposal procedures comply with the law.

- **Theft** This should cover everything – stock, plant and equipment. Essential if you are in retail.
- **Motor insurance** Required by law for any vehicle; business-class insurance is required by law for any vehicles used primarily for business. This includes private cars used by salespeople or other employees who are constantly on the road.
- **Employee fraud (fidelity guarantee)** Essential where employees handle money on behalf of the company. The insurance will be compromised if the employer does not carry out strict and full security checks on each employee.
- **Professional liability insurance** Protects against negligent, inadequate or dishonest professional advice. Professional bodies will not accept you as a member if you do not have this insurance.
- **Intellectual copyright insurance** Covers abuse of copyright, patents, licences and trademarks.
- **Computer virus/malicious erasure/hacking cover** Vital if you are in e-commerce. At the time of writing, insurance companies are still unsure about this sort of cover and some include it as part of other policies.
- **Internet risks** Packages cover damage to third-party software or hardware caused by downloading a virus; breach of data protection legislation by hackers; infringement of copyright or other intellectual property; financial loss from third-party fraud; business interruption due to web site failure; and loss arising from a third party gaining access to customer data.
- **Engineering insurance** Protects selected plant against accidental damage and breakdown, but is compromised if you do not carry out regular inspections.
- **Latent defects** Ten-year cover for new structures, offered by only a few insurance companies. It is subject to rigorous building inspection while the structure is being erected.
- **Product recall** Insurance against the cost of locating and recalling products that are found to be defective or hazardous.
- **Product guarantee** Covers costs arising out of a product's failure to meet specifications.

- **Product liability** To protect against any harm being caused to a third party by a company's product.
- **Product tamper and extortion** Covers malicious interference with a company's products or assets.
- **Director's and officer's personal liability insurance** Protects against a breach of duty by a company's senior officers.
- **Death in service benefits** Usually part of a personal accident policy provided to employees.
- **Key man insurance** Protects against the death of an essential senior member of staff.
- **Health insurances** Critical illness cover pays out a tax-free lump sum on diagnosis of a life-threatening illness. Income replacement cover (also known as permanent health insurance) makes monthly payments – typically 50 per cent of a policy-holder's net income – to employees unable to work, possibly up to retirement. Long-term care cover covers younger people who develop an illness which requires long-term care in a care facility, or can be linked to a pension scheme to provide long-term care for retired employees in an old people's home.
- **Credit insurance** Relevant if you do business with trade customers. Protects against bad debts from other businesses.

Reviewing your insurance needs

As part of risk assessment, insurance cover should be reassessed at frequent intervals. Most insurance companies insist that this is done annually but it is more advisable to do so at least every six months. The major insurers and broking houses have risk evaluation teams who will willingly undertake an audit of your company's position and will also advise on where changes need to be made in company procedures in order to secure firm insurance cover for any eventuality.

As technology increasingly takes over in the world of business, it exposes companies to as many risks as it does benefits. Most of the concerns about liability and protection are generated by the poor security record of many computer systems. Some fairly large companies have suffered, at the least, acute embarrassment over breaches in their security systems and, at the worst, major financial losses.

For detailed information on insurance, read *The Which? Guide to Insurance* from Which? Books.*

Chapter 14

Looking after yourself and your staff

It is important to maintain a work-life balance at all times, and especially when under pressure. This chapter explains how to look after yourself and maintain a healthy perspective on your business. It also looks at your obligations towards staff and how to prevent work-related illness.

Avoiding work-related problems

The 24-hour society has become a reality. The dominance of technology means that business has become a global interaction and, consequently, traditional working times have become redundant. A report by Incomes Data Services (IDS) in April 2000 predicted serious health consequences as a result of people being employed outside standard working hours, and noted that many companies no longer have a 'normal' working day. With the demise of the nine to five, there is a risk that business concerns may intrude around the clock. Combined with increasing pressure at work and the need to work long hours, the workforce runs the risk of stress, depression and tiredness.

Long hours

Britons work the longest hours in Europe, and take less holiday than their European counterparts. Nearly a third of senior full-time employees work more than 46 hours a week, and senior managers often work more than 51 hours. A survey by *Director* magazine and consultants KPMG in 2000 found that directors commonly worked 51–60 hours per week and that totals of more than 60 hours were more prevalent amongst directors of SMEs.

It can be easy to slip into workaholism, but working longer hours is no guarantee of getting a lot done – instead, it is more likely that productivity and morale will decline. The business writer Charles Handy outlines the dangers in his article *Living fast, dying rich*: 'Even without falling prey to depression, 80-hour weeks are no better for senior executives than they are for junior doctors. Both can make false diagnoses and wrong prescriptions when suffering from extreme weariness. The symptoms of tired behaviour are well established; it isn't the bleary eyes or the dropping jaw, it's the imperative to make things simple in order to operate. We do this by polarising issues into black and white, right or wrong, no greys or in-betweens; we do it by stereotyping people and situations to fit them into familiar boxes which we know how to deal with; we shorten the time horizons and postpone all the difficult decisions until another day.'

Time pressure can be a major source of stress at work, and many people feel compelled to work longer hours in order to keep up. If not properly managed, this can cause psychological and physical illness and affect personal relationships. In a 1999 survey conducted by the Institute of Management called *The Quality of Working Life*, 71 per cent of owner/managers reported that working long hours had an adverse impact on their health, 79 per cent said that it affected their relationship with their spouse/partner, and 86 per cent said that it had a negative effect on their relationship with their children.

By getting organised and working more efficiently, it is possible to stay on top of the workload and prevent the need to work long hours. A number of time management techniques can be employed to streamline everyday office tasks. These include using technology such as email appropriately (see page 179), delegating effectively, tackling paperwork (for example, pruning documentation and instituting an organised filing system) and cutting down on interruptions. It can also help to prioritise your objectives in order to devote more time to the things that you really want to do. Chapter 4 gives general suggestions on procedures that will help you run your business more effectively, while outsourcing functions to relieve the administrative burden is described on pages 117 and 185.

Stress

A certain amount of stress can improve performance. However, too much pressure can cause physical and emotional ill health and lead to burnout. In Japan, where workaholism is enshrined in the culture, there is a word – *karoshi* – to describe death caused by overwork. While *karoshi* is not common in the UK, work-related stress is, and contributes towards levels of absenteeism (see page 169).

SMEs face many key issues and challenges every day. Sometimes, these issues can quickly degenerate into fears, which can accumulate as the business comes up against yet more red tape, or a member of staff decides to take the company to an employment tribunal. The 'sue-you' culture has become increasingly vicious, and many employers are overly nervous of litigious employees – some rightly so. Many owner/managers seem to be in a permanent state of tension and unable to unwind.

About 40 per cent of working people felt they were under excessive pressure in January 2001, according to the International Stress Management Association. As well as the cost to health, stress also takes its toll on the economy. Each year stress-related illness costs the UK £3.9bn, and the US 10 per cent of its gross national product.

Symptoms of stress include:

- constant tiredness but inability to sleep properly at night
- lack of appetite or constant craving for sugary foods or caffeine to give energy levels a quick boost
- depression and/or anxiety
- depression of the immune system, leading to an increased number of viruses and conditions such as arthritis, irritable bowel syndrome and allergic disorders
- shortness of breath and/or chest pains
- irritability
- lack of concentration
- headaches.

It can help simply to stand back and analyse the situation. Some stress is attitudinal and caused by a feeling of being out of control. Identifying the factors that are behind the stress and determining strategies to alleviate it may drastically reduce the problem before you even have a chance to put your plans into action. Other ways of coping are to remove or lessen the cause of stress. For example, if you are feeling overburdened, look at ways of reducing your work-load or hire extra staff. If you are finding work difficult, tell some-one or get help. Executive coaches have sprung up in recent years to meet the needs of pressured owner/managers (see page 218). For more advice on combatting stress, see *The Which? Guide to Managing Stress* from Which? Books.★

Depression

Research in 1999 by American scientists working on behalf of the US government estimated that depression at work was costing the US $56bn a year – roughly the same amount as heart disease. However, heart disease in the US and in the UK is often covered by private company health plans. Depression is not, and usually ends up costing the company because of the poor quality of work a depressed person produces and absenteeism.

Worrying about work can be a factor in depression. In the *Quality of Working Life* survey (see page 199) 52 per cent of respondents were worried about job security; 58 per cent said that their employers expected them to work long hours; and 60 per cent said they felt guilty about being off work when they were ill.

Depression is a treatable condition. In mild cases, counselling may help. Other instances may involve the prescription of medication or a stay in hospital. Your GP will be able to refer you for appropriate treatment, while the British Association for Counselling and Psychotherapy★ can supply a list of counsellors in your area.

Tiredness

One possible effect of the 24-hour society is a permanent state of tiredness among workers. The Sleep Research Laboratory at Loughborough University attributes sleep deficit to the 'macho, long-hours working culture'. Sleep deprivation, which is more often caused by poor quality of sleep than not enough hours in bed, can severely impair people's ability to sustain attention and plan effectively, and can affect speech and memory patterns and flexible thinking. In a worst-case scenario it can lead to fatal accidents in the workplace.

Poor quality of sleep is often caused by not going to bed in a relaxed state. Not getting enough sleep can increase the chances of being trapped in a cycle of fatigue and insomnia, since people who are tired have to work harder to keep up during the day.

These approaches can help to overcome sleep problems:

- treat any underlying disease
- exercise regularly, but not just before going to bed
- avoid caffeine, smoking and alcohol, especially before bedtime
- use relaxation and breathing techniques and try to wind down before going to bed (e.g. not spending hours in front of the computer)
- keep the bedroom free of distractions such as a computer or television, and make it a comfortable, welcoming environment
- try not to read business papers in bed
- adopt a regular sleep routine, going to bed and getting up at roughly the same time each day.

These techniques can aid a good night's rest, dispel fatigue and enhance performance during the day. The Royal College of Psychiatrists★ has produced *Sleeping Well*, a patient information leaflet which can be ordered from the organisation or downloaded from its web site.

Creating a work–life balance

The cost of long hours, stress and tiredness does not just affect businesses, it is also impacts on the family. According to government statistics in 2001, one in three fathers regularly works a ten-hour day (excluding the daily commute). Many men are unable to devote as much time as they would like to their children in the evening – helping with homework, say, or being involved in after-school activities like football clubs or youth groups. However, it is not just men who are under pressure. More women are working than ever before. Working mothers, who have to juggle the often conflicting demands of career and family, are a particularly time-deprived group.

These trends have had an effect on the wider community. Many villages within commuting distance of major towns are deserted during the daytime.

The government is trying to assist in resolving work-related health problems. Throughout 2000 the DfEE* and the Women's Unit surveyed 7,500 employees and 2,500 employers. The report found that:

- one in eight employees reported working on both Saturdays and Sundays
- one in five employees worked for companies that were open 24 hours a day, seven days a week
- employees were more likely to be offered stress counselling to help with the effects of long-hours culture than be offered assistance with their basic childcare needs
- 80 per cent of the workplaces surveyed had employees who worked more than the standard hours and 39 per cent of those did so without extra pay.

The report, which had a special focus on working women, recommended flexible working practices as a means of resolving health problems and helping working mothers to cope. Flexible working can allow people to fulfil family commitments and dictate hours that suit them (see page 164). The government has expressed its approval of flexible working since it can lead to a happier, healthier workforce and bottom-line benefits for the employer. It also means that employers can accommodate staff from different backgrounds and therefore widen the 'pool' of potential skills.

Improving the work environment

Sometimes the surroundings at work constitute a health hazard. Working for up to eight hours a day hunched over a computer terminal has been identified as a cause of many musculoskeletal disorders. These disorders account for 40 to 50 per cent of all work-related sickness, according to the European Agency for Safety and Health at Work. Typing at a keyboard for intensive periods and having to use poorly designed office equipment may also cause repetitive strain injury (RSI), also known as work-related upper limb disorder.

Since 1992 regulations have required companies to undertake risk assessments for their office employees and advise them on health issues. To improve employees' working conditions – and possibly avoid litigation (see page 217) – employers should consider implementing the following health and safety measures:

- equip employees with properly designed workstations and office furniture
- install adequate lighting and ventilation
- maintain equipment and power services in a safe condition
- introduce better company practices, such as encouraging work breaks away from the keyboard (perhaps via a regular flashing message on screen), and reinforce the message through education
- get experts to adjust the lighting and humidity to protect employees' eyes. Screen breaks should be taken to rest the eyes (every 15 minutes is recommended) and employees should be advised to blink their eyes regularly and to drink lots of water. You could offer free sight tests (these are required by law for monitor users)
- increase staff awareness of health and safety issues through communication initiatives and training.

The Health and Safety Executive (HSE)★ can advise on carrying out a risk assessment and provide further information about safety in the workplace.

Survival tips for employers

You have an obligation towards your employees. However, only you can take responsibility for your own mental and physical well-being. Many owner/managers find that after the first few years have passed and they have devoted everything to building up their business, it is no longer necessary to live every working day in an 'adrenaline rush'. It is sometimes impossible for individuals to calm down, pull back from the business and devote some time to themselves and their family.

In order to develop the art of relaxation while not dropping the reins altogether, you have to learn to do the following:

- develop trust in your managers
- delegate
- concentrate on your special skills in the business
- take time off

- organise your life into segments
- set yourself personal targets
- ask for help if you need it
- look after your mental health
- look after your physical health
- develop time management skills.

Develop trust in your managers

It is strongly advisable to develop teamwork and be able to trust your management team to do the best for your company in your absence. Some entrepreneurs are unable to let other people get on with their jobs without feeling the need to check on their work and intervene, which can cause problems.

Most successful business people tend to be very talented, particularly those with wide experience of an industry. For example, someone who has worked his or her way up from the shop floor of a manufacturing company and was either part of a management buy-out or created a company in the same sector would have an invaluable store of knowledge, which would be useful to the company and the employees. However, some owner/managers with this sort of experience and ability are reluctant to trust anyone else to perform certain tasks because they feel they can do the job better.

In order to develop a good relationship with your managers, you have to show them that you are happy to trust them by giving them special responsibilities and allowing them a certain amount of self-sufficiency. They are likely to function better without interruption, while you can help to ensure peace of mind by developing effective communication networks and asking to be kept up to date on developments.

Delegate

People who do not delegate put themselves under a great deal of stress. Some employers are reluctant to assign tasks to others because they consider that employees will not do the job as well as they would, or are even incompetent. However, others are unlikely to be inept – they may simply have different working methods. Sensible employers recognise that other people have their own, equally successful ways of operating and offer them tasks that play to their strengths.

Another reason for not delegating is to maintain appearances. Perhaps you feel that if you do not show everyone that you are a superman or -woman, they will think less of you. You might consider that this is perfectionism: 'No one does the job as well as I do.' However, this sort of attitude can signify insecurity, and mean that you end up overloading yourself with work. Of course, it is important that a good entrepreneur has his or her finger on the pulse of the business at all times and is aware of all the details of the company and its operations. This does not mean having a finger in every pie. You would not employ an accountant and then do the books yourself (although it would be permissable to check them now and then). Similarly, you may set personnel policy but would be advised to leave the fine detail of staff contracts to human resources.

Concentrate on your special skills in the business

You should concentrate on what you are best at – developing your business. It was your business instinct that got the business off the ground in the first place. You are where you are today because of your acumen, flair, nose for a marketing opportunity, networking ability, creativity, specialist skills (scientific/engineering/IT) and ability to raise finance. Whatever your personal strengths are, focus on them. Leave functions which are not really your forte, or which hold you back, to other people. Follow the principles of the large businesses that stripped back to their core activities and outsourced the rest to competent employees in order to regenerate themselves. Do *not* try and do it all yourself. There may have been a time when you did – when you had to – because your business was small. One of the luxuries of business success is that you can pay other people to do things for you.

Take time off

You are not letting anyone down by taking time off. Nor is the business going to collapse if you are away for a week. It is important to take a break from the pressures of work now and then. No one advocates the kind of 'absentee owner' lifestyle cultivated by some chief executives who can more easily be found on the golf course than in their own offices. However, the danger of never taking a break is that you will eventually become jaded and lose your sense of perspective, which could result in inappropriate decisions as well as a cost to physical and mental health.

Taking a break means, sometimes, a *complete break*. No mobile phones, no laptops, no sending and receiving emails before taking breakfast by the pool. No leaving your mobile constantly switched on all through that cruise down the Nile. As mentioned above, it is important to be able to trust your employees and delegate effectively. Owner/managers who genuinely believe that their staff are going to bankrupt them, set fire to the place, embezzle company funds or alienate all the customers the moment their backs are turned are likely to be most in need of a holiday. Employers who suffer from extreme anxiety should contact their GP or seek psychological help.

Organise your life into segments

Letting your business dominate your life to the extent that you have no social or family life is unlikely to be a recipe for fulfilment. A growing number of business people who spend long hours in the office find it difficult to find a partner, and dating agencies have sprung up in recent years to cater specifically for busy executives. Leaving work behind in social situations may be the best recipe for success. The owner of one dating agency in London that went bust commented: 'It was a big mistake concentrating on this marketplace. We would set up dinner parties for 10 to 12 business people, so that they could meet that special someone, and half of them wouldn't turn up, pleading that they had business emergencies at the last minute. The half that did turn up would spend all evening talking about their business, taking calls on their mobile phones and sending emails on their WAP phones.'

Try to compartmentalise your life, so you can put aside business concerns when you are out of the office and devote yourself fully to family and friends. *Which? Way to Manage Your Time – and your Life*, from Which? Books,* explains how to define your priorities and take control so that work does not rule your personal life.

Set yourself personal targets

It is a good idea to have an ambition in life outside of your business, and to cherish personal goals which mean as much to you as your company does. It can be helpful to write down what you want to achieve and develop a personal mission statement that sums up your aims and philosophy on life.

Being devoted to your business does not mean that you cannot find a little bit of passion for a hobby. If you set yourself some goals and establish how to meet them, you will assist your self-development and quite possibly obtain a new perspective on your business. For example, you might have always wanted to learn to play the piano so could take lessons once a week in your lunch hour. Alternatively, if scuba diving is your ambition, you could investigate courses at your local swimming pool. It is important to enjoy your work, but you should be able to obtain satisfaction and happiness from other activities.

Ask for help if you need it

It can be lonely at the top, especially if you are in need of advice. Sometimes it is difficult to talk to colleagues, who may not have the necessary expertise to assist you. If you own the business, you may not want to give the impression that you are not strong, in control, totally organised and able to get the best out of yourself and your workforce. It can be hard to talk to a partner at home because he or she may not fully understand the various pressures of the business and is likely to be biased towards the work–life ratio being tilted heavily in favour of the 'life' side.

Management consultants have invented the 'executive coach' (or life coach) to meet the needs of business people. An executive coach is a mentor figure who aims to help you adjust your work–life ratio, decrease your stress levels and help with time management. He or she can provide just the sympathetic but firm ear that a busy executive needs. Executive coaches are consultants who understand fully the day-to-day business climate as well as their clients' personal needs. They can help people to deal with specific projects or problems or clarify their values, and will assist with brainstorming and drawing up a plan of action.

Executive coaches teach their clients to recognise traits that may have an adverse effect on themselves or other people, such as workaholism or finding it difficult to relinquish control. They help executives to spot when their behaviour is making other staff unhappy, and encourage them to reassess their personal and work-related values and goals.

Business owners can also demand one-to-one attention when trying to look after their health. According to experts in the business press, the biggest growth industry of the 21st century after childcare is the personal trainer or gym coach (see page 218).

Look after your mental health

The Institute of Directors (IoD)★ estimates that owner-managed and entrepreneurial business forms approximately 75 per cent of Britain's business community. Many people among this sizeable percentage are struggling against sometimes overwhelming odds, and in the face of myriad business pressures it is vital to take care of one's mental well-being.

Try to guard against normal *concerns* in your working life becoming *fears*. You can go some way towards this by taking the advice in this chapter and trying to keep things in perspective. If you, or those close to you, recognise that your perceptions have changed, your confidence seems dimmed or you have adopted an unrealistic or extreme approach, it is time to pull right back for a while and allow your mind to recover from stress. When anxiety takes over, you have to seek help.

Look after your physical health

Mental health is invariably tied up with physical health. Many executives have an erratic lifestyle involving insufficient sleep, a sedentary existence and poor eating habits. Frequent meetings, business trips and long hours can all take a toll on your health. If you fail to maintain a balanced lifestyle, you may become run down and compromise the success of your enterprise. To ensure that you look after yourself and obtain peak performance, follow the advice below.

- If you must make a very early start, have a substantial breakfast within one hour of rising to stabilise your blood sugar levels. Avoid fried food.
- Drink plenty of water, preferably bottled mineral water, throughout the day. Two litres a day is recommended.

- Cut down on coffee and tea.
- Stop smoking, or cut down.
- Eat at least five portions of fruit and vegetables a day to maintain adequate levels of vitamins and other minerals.
- Avoid large lunches, which can make you feel sluggish in the afternoon.
- Eat regular meals. Do not skip meals.
- Small amounts of wine can be good for the heart, but drink more water to counteract the dehydrating effects of alcohol.
- Take regular moderate exercise – 20 minutes three times a week is recommended. Swimming, walking and cycling are all beneficial forms of exercise. The activity should be gentle but aerobic enough to make you puff a bit. Exercising infrequently and over-exerting yourself is not advisable (e.g. avoid torturing yourself on the squash court once a month).
- Try to cut down on meetings, and avoid being sedentary for prolonged periods of time. Move around after an hour of sitting down to get your circulation going again and to improve your posture.
- Cut down on unnecessary air travel. The recirculated air in the cabin harbours viruses and makes your eyes dry, you get a dose of radiation every time you fly, and entering different time zones disturbs your body clock. To reduce the risk of deep vein thrombosis on long-haul journeys you should exercise in your seat or walk around during the flight.
- Ideally, do not work at a computer for more than one hour without having a break.
- Try not to take work home and allow time for relaxation.

Business executives may manage companies but often do not devote as much time as they should to managing themselves. Looking after yourself is common sense, and means spending time on number one.

Develop time management skills

You have to make time. Time for conversations, time for thinking, time for looking for something in the shops, time for booking a holiday, time for buying someone a birthday present, time for your children, time for yourself and time for your business.

You should make the decision to allocate time for these things *willingly*, not resentfully or grudgingly. Your business will occupy a very large part of your day but it should not occupy every waking hour. You have to decide which parts of your life belong to which times of the day and be rigid about keeping the different sections free most of the time. For example, you could decide that Sunday is to be totally devoted to your family/yourself/your partner/your elderly mother/your hobby, and that only an emergency (a *real* emergency) is allowed to interrupt it. To manage time effectively, such rules are important.

Time management is also about negotiating agreements with others. With your partner, for example, you could agree that perhaps you might have to work on Saturday mornings but that it will never spill over into Saturday afternoons. His or her part of the agreement might be to accept the Saturday mornings and not object, nag or be upset so long as you keep your part of the agreement for the rest of Saturday. Similarly, you could agree that you will not work late more than two nights a week and set aside at least one night to spend time with your partner in a one-to-one situation – no children, no friends, just the two of you.

Time management for yourself might mean that you free up two lunchtimes a week for going swimming or pursuing another activity that gives your mind and body a boost. Essentially, you need to change your life so that you are proactive (making the decisions, allocating the time and managing your life) rather than reactive (rushing along from one 'crisis' to another, being pulled this way and that by the demands of work and home and perhaps always promising that when this particular period is over you will make more time for things). Being more disciplined about time and making choices will enable you to feel empowered. For more advice on ways to manage yourself successfully, see *Which? Way to Manage your Time – and Your Life*, from Which Books.*

Chapter 15

What the future holds

The prospects for small businesses are affected by the performance of the economy, legislative changes and general social trends. This chapter looks at some of the major developments likely to affect SMEs.

A positive climate for business

At the time of writing, the UK's economy was shaky due to a 'will we – won't we' relationship with the single currency. Growth in the economy decelerated sharply to its slowest for two years in the last quarter of 2000, and the UK was over £660 billion in debt, partly as a result of reliance on credit-card borrowing. However, all is not gloom.

According to research carried out by the analysts GrowthPlus in conjunction with the management consultant firm Arthur Andersen, Britain is the best place in the world to set up a business. At the time of its publication in January 2001, the report's authors reckoned that tax, employment and welfare laws in the UK were the most business-friendly in the world – even ahead of the US. Other European countries fell well behind. The report ranked ten major world economies according to ease of obtaining investment, the amount of government red tape and the availability of skilled labour. Among the top three, Britain scored 49 out of 60, the US 45, and Spain 43; Sweden came last with 34.

The authors commented that Britain was doing more than most countries to stimulate business growth and a dynamic economy, and that other countries should follow its example in rewarding enterprise. Only two European countries – Britain and France – provide tax incentives or a special tax regime for private investors.

A national strategy for SMEs

In October 2000, the Small Business Service (SBS)★ launched two consultation documents designed to affect radically the business environment for SMEs. *Integrating the Business Support Infrastructure for SMEs* outlines the government's intention to provide a national framework that supports small business through access to funding, especially private venture capital. In this initiative the government hopes to encourage workforce developments, reduce the risks involved in setting up and running a business and promote a more entrepreneurial culture.

Think Small First contains the first-ever national strategy for supporting SMEs in the UK. It promises that administrative procedures will be streamlined without going into too much detail about how this will be accomplished, although there are references to 'networks of advice', 'easing administrative burdens' and 'continual consultation with business'. Two statements, however, have a more solid feel to them. One is the undertaking to promote entrepreneurial skills in young people by a process of collaboration between the education system and business. The other is the intention to take a more commercially focused approach to finance and to attract significant amounts of risk capital to the private sector, particularly for small innovative businesses. This could signify that the government is less likely to give grants to businesses in future. The document also discusses rescue and reconstruction mechanisms for failing businesses.

It is difficult to tell how any of these initiatives might work in practice, or whether they will be implemented. None of the measures proposed in both documents is particularly concrete and at the time of writing, the government was approaching a General Election.

Impending bureaucracy from Brussels

However many helpful initiatives are in place to promote and guide business, the red tape must still be dealt with. Most bureaucracy emanates from the EU, and a number of forthcoming directives could have implications for SMEs in the UK.

One of the biggest shake-ups may be on the pensions front, with the introduction of stakeholder pensions by the British government (see page 182). In addition, European Commissioners want to create a pan-European market so that financial services companies can sell pensions across national borders. In order to achieve this, they are formulating an agreed set of solvency rules and other technical provisions. This would mean a major reorganisation of the UK private pensions system which, experts say, could lead to companies ceasing to offer pay-linked pensions. Other EU countries have, according to the government departments dealing with EU legislation, fallen a long way behind the UK in the development of private-sector pension funding and it has been suggested that the UK could end up losing out as a result of the EU formulating legislation to allow the others to catch up. The Department of Social Security (DSS) intends to study the EU proposals carefully before looking at how they will affect the UK.

In January 2001 there was a debate between the UK government and industry over the failure of the government to reduce the burden of regulation on new and small businesses. The Director General of the British Chambers of Commerce argued that the current Labour government had raised business taxation by £10bn during its term of office, and that the EU was not doing enough to lighten the burden of regulations on start-up companies. Even the European Parliament has prepared a report which says that Brussels needs to speed up and strengthen a scheme designed to simplify European legislation.

In the same month, millions of pounds were spent by the British government on mailing letters to businesses urging them to sign up to the euro. At the time of writing, the Treasury's Euro Preparations Unit, which costs the taxpayer £27m to fund, was urging businesses to download the euro symbol from the EU web site and to use it on their company literature and letterheads. It also warned all businesses that by January 2002 all firms in the euro area, which comprises 12 European countries, will have to deal in the euro. After this date, electronic payments in the present European currencies will no longer be available. At the time of writing, British businesses, which were awaiting either a referendum or a change of government, appeared to not be responding to this warning.

There are other worries on the horizon for businesses. The 'Information in Advance' Directive is currently under way in Brussels. When implemented, it will require businesses to consult with their employees or employee representatives in advance over any form of action being considered that might affect employment within a company. In other words, if a business was considering a merger, takeover or acquisition it would have to consult with employees and/or their unions before taking any action. Although the wording of the draft directive is vague, it is the fear of businesses (and the hope of trade union leaders) that it signals a future where businesses are managed by negotiation between unions and employers, not by decisions of the Board.

Experts predict that if this directive were adopted it would dramatically cut the flow of investment from foreign companies in the UK. At present, one of the attractions of the UK is that it is perceived to have a business culture in which companies can make decisions to expand, contract or develop their business as market conditions dictate. The directive would limit such freedoms. If owners/managers were required by law to consult with employees over their plans it might mean that deals could only be accomplished much more slowly. Competitive advantages may be lost, companies could lose share value while negotiations went on, and any element of confidentiality might be compromised. Adoption of the directive could lead to employees and/or unions vetoing company development plans if they did not feel that the move was in their best interests – effectively a case of the tail wagging the dog. Of course, employee concerns should not be ignored. However, from an employer's perspective, staff may not be able to understand the complexities of company growth and will only be able to see the short-term picture. British businesses, judging by the flurry of activity and objections that this proposed directive has created, do not feel confident in the representation being made to Brussels on their behalf by the UK government.

Finding and keeping employees in future

Pending legislation is not the only problem that British businesses will have to face in the future. Skill shortages (see page 161) can only get worse in the short term while the Department for Education and Employment (DfEE)* continues to struggle to create the right education system to feed the nation's businesses in the future. Already, many of Britain's brightest and best are being persuaded to take their talents elsewhere in Europe. The year 2000 and early months of 2001 have seen a concerted effort in some quarters to encourage students to study and work in Europe. Several directories of career opportunities in Europe have been launched along with numerous web sites, and conferences are aimed at A-level and GNVQ students interested in pursuing European careers and education opportunities. Those skilled workers who do stay in the UK are becoming more demanding over employment packages.

The employment package

The perks have to be very juicy in order to tempt some high-flyers into certain jobs. Salary may not be as important as fringe benefits which enable employees to plan for the future or safeguard their health (such as pension schemes, share options and medical insurance). However, a survey by Hays Management Consultants, conducted in 2000, concluded that share options have become useless as a means of attracting new staff to Internet start-ups, following the demise of many dotcom companies. Many cash-poor e-businesses previously relied on share options as a useful tool to keep salaries down. They are now raising their pay levels far beyond the national average (9.7 per cent compared with 3.6 per cent for the industrial and service sectors) in order to attract and keep staff.

Employee insurance packages have become an issue for companies seeking to attract new workers, particularly since the National Health Service is perceived to be declining and unreliable. Employees not only want medical insurance packages to cover their immediate family but want add-ons such as critical illness cover, income replacement and long-term care cover (see page 197).

Whether or not a job is acceptable may all come down to how easy it is for individuals to accommodate their lifestyle. Research in 2000 by the personal services provider Ten UK showed that, given a choice between more money or a better balance between work and social life, most graduates would choose the latter. Flexible working may represent an attractive option to many employees (see Chapter 11).

Pension schemes

The quality of a pension scheme is deemed to be an important part of an employee package. More and more employees are claiming that traditional pension rules – where the pension is paid only to a lawfully wedded spouse when a scheme member dies – are not good enough. Companies are now under pressure to consider adding unmarried (including homosexual) partners to the payout. The Inland Revenue (IR)* has decreed that schemes may pay a pension to someone other than a lawful spouse providing the couple can prove financial interdependency. This means proving that the couple live together and share financial arrangements such as a mortgage, bank accounts, council tax and utility bills. Several large companies, such as British Airways and British Telecom, have already embraced the new culture. The Post Office will pay a pension to an employee's carer, if, say, a son or daughter can show that they gave up work to care for their relative and were dependent upon the sick employee's pension. Death in service benefits (see page 197) are usually paid at the trustees' discretion but in practice will be paid to anyone an employee nominates.

The rise of the compensation culture

The future does not promise any relief from employees suing employers, regardless of whether their complaints are justified. Many employers are fearful because some workers feel that they have the right to sue over anything. New legislation has raised the maximum amount an employee can win for unfair dismissal to over £50,000 (with no limit at all in health and safety cases). In 1999 there were 167,354 actions against employers – an increase of 27 per cent, according to the Advisory, Conciliation and Arbitration Service (ACAS).* A recent spate of court awards for stress-related illnesses have opened up the field even further.

The modern workplace – particularly the office environment, which is less regulated than the manufacturing environment – can give rise to all kinds of health issues, which employers should be aware of (see page 203). Many smaller companies skip the obligation to comply with health regulations and, as a result, make themselves vulnerable to having lawsuits for work-related illness or injury slapped on them.

Insurance companies may dictate the policies of the future in this area. Some insurance companies are now putting pressure on their clients to reduce their health and legal bills – as well as the potential for any large payouts – by insisting that offices are equipped with properly designed workstations, adequate lighting and ventilation, and that they display better company practice over health issues. Some American companies have even set up in-house gymnasiums where employees are required to take a 15-minute brisk walk on a treadmill or do some rowing exercises to eliminate the kind of musculoskeletal disorders that result from a sedentary workstyle.

The modern disease of stress has now been recognised by the courts. Its causes and ways to reduce it in the workplace are discussed on pages 200–1. In future it is likely that employers will have to guard against employees with stress-related conditions claiming against them by following two paths. First, employers will have to make the application procedure for potential employees much more rigorous in order to weed out the employees who will not be able to handle the normal level of stress the job entails. For years, consultants have advocated psychometric testing as part of the interviewing procedure. These are written tests drawn up by psychologists which claim to show the true facets of an applicant's personality. It is difficult, but not impossible, to try to determine whether an interviewee will really be able to cope when the chips are down.

Second, employers will have to do all they can to minimise the stress levels of employees with major demands on their personal lives – such as children, elderly dependants and divorce or separation problems. This can be achieved by adopting an open mind about flexible working, either in order to allow an employee to adjust his or her life in the short term, or as a long-term option. More and more companies see this as the way of the future, and it can enhance productivity. The advantages are also personal. Achieving a better work–life balance benefits everyone, including senior management.

The growth of specialist consultants

Many people find that they do not have the time to make mentoring relationships with people that they know, or to fit in regular exercise. It is now possible to pay someone to be your guide, therapist and teacher. Recent years have seen the development of a growth industry in personal consultation services. Executive coaches help business people to develop time management skills, and equip them to face new challenges or deal with crises (see page 208). Meanwhile, time-hungry entrepreneurs who want to get the most out of their gym sessions are turning increasingly to personal trainers. A personal trainer will devise a structured, personalised exercise plan for each individual and offer motivation and support. Personal trainers advertise locally, but many prefer to rent time in a gym where clients can buy one-to-one coaching by the hour.

The demand for ethics

One of the better developments at the start of the 21st century is the rediscovery of the collective conscience and the growing focus on ethics. This could have far-reaching implications for business.

In recent years, consumers have become increasingly concerned that commercial enterprises and industry should adhere to ethical principles. According to the national press in 2000, 50 per cent of the general public boycotted a product or company because they did not approve of how that company did business or where and how it made its products. This ranged from people not buying chocolate produced using slave labour, to boycotting trainers made in the developing world by eight-year-old children and taking a stand against genetically modified (GM) food.

Many companies have found, to their cost, that pursuing unethical activities can taint their reputation if not their market value. In 2001, the Church of England removed the major conglomerate GKN from its share portfolio after publicity about GKN's involvement in the arms trade. At the time of writing, a company called Huntingdon Life Sciences had just been saved from bankruptcy by an anonymous American investor, who bailed the business out when all its British investors backed out due to pressure from animal rights groups.

Many instances exist of ethical concerns dictating to business – for example, witness the rapid growth of the market for organic food. All the major supermarkets now have organic ranges, and many consumers are prepared to pay more for organic produce. The food retailer Iceland was the first to refuse to have anything to do with GM products, and its subsequent success was attributed to this stance. It is now attempting gradually to make all of its lines organic. Products ranging from coffee and chocolate to washing powder are marketed on the grounds that they do not harm the environment or the local economy. Some carry the Fairtrade mark, which symbolises to consumers that the company is committed to guaranteeing a better deal for farmers in the developing world.

Figures put out by the Ethical Investment Research Information Service show that retail ethical figures are doubling every three years. At the time of writing, the market in ethical goods is worth £3.3 billion.

Ethical demands are even making inroads, albeit in a small way, into the financial services market. 'Green' mortgages are currently available from the Co-operative Bank and the Norwich and Peterborough Building Society. As part of their mortgage schemes both companies pledge to a programme of reforestation: the Co-operative Bank subscribes to Climate Care, a scheme which plants forests in Uganda to combat global warming, while the Norwich and Peterborough Building Society aims to create forests in East Anglia and Lincolnshire. The Ecology Building Society (the second fastest-growing building society in the UK in 1999) is the only society at the time of writing to provide mortgages for eco-friendly self-build or reclamation projects.

From July 2000, all occupational pension scheme trustees must include in their statement of investment principles a reference to ethical investment, stating the extent to which (if at all) they take social, environmental or ethical considerations into account. This practice has been a major force for change in the US.

There is no doubt that ethical considerations will play a bigger part in the business policies of the future.

Technological developments

Email, videoconferencing, personal information managers (PIMs) and palmtop computers are just some of the innovations that have helped business people to communicate more effectively and get organised in recent years. The future promises new developments that will assist with personal time management, enable new marketing initiatives and streamline business functions.

The Internet offers many opportunities to small businesses, but embracing e-commerce is no guarantee of success. Some companies which got their fingers burnt on the Web have reverted to old-fashioned marketing initiatives. Chapter 5 looks at the prospects for businesses selling on the Internet in more detail.

The developing field of m-commerce offers some interesting possibilities. For example, future house-hunters might access property information on a WAP phone while they are out and about looking for their new home. Mobile phones will soon be manufactured with locating devices imbedded in them so that people can be found in an emergency – a boon to the emergency services. Meanwhile the development of the mobile tour guide is likely, with people being able to access a complete information service about their current location via their phone. Experts predict that the days are not far off when people will be able to watch downloaded videos through special glasses plugged into a WAP phone, or check their blood pressure through their mobile. For more on m-commerce see page 84.

Avoiding the pressure

The advances described above undoubtedly spell new opportunities for business, but may have a down side. While some people relish the exciting, high-speed cutting edge of technology, others envisage a frightening spiral down into a society where pressure is intense and people never get away from work.

Imagine a typical working day in the future. While you are waiting for the train to the office in the morning you might check your emails, then do your banking. While you are on the train you could have a videoconference with two of your salespeople in other parts of the country. You might then go into your company's intranet system read some reports and check the company noticeboard. Before the train arrives, you might have time to check your blood pressure and order a taxi to meet you at the station on your mobile phone. And all that just on the way to the office – the working day lies ahead.

Some people might predict that the biggest growth industry in the next ten years is going to be selling uninhabited islands to busy executives in desperate need of escape. With the increased pace of work, it is even more important to look after your health and maintain a balanced lifestyle. By following the advice in this book, you should be able to stay on top of things and make the best decisions for your business.

Addresses

The Advisory, Conciliation and Arbitration Service (ACAS)
Brandon House
180 Borough High Street
London SE1 1LW
Tel: 020-7386 5100
Web site: *www.acas.org.uk*

Anglia Business Associates (ABA) Ltd
4 Penfold Drive
Gateway 11
Business Park
Wymondham
Norfolk NR18 0WZ
Tel: (01953) 600811
Fax: (01953) 600822

The Arts Council of England
14 Great Peter Street
London SW1P 3NQ
Tel: 020-7973 6517
Fax: 020-7973 6590
Email: enquiries@artscouncil.org.uk
Web site: *www.artscouncil.org.uk*

Banking Ombudsman Scheme (BOS)
See Financial Ombudsman Service

Association of Chartered Certified Accountants
29 Lincoln's Inn Fields
London WC2A 3EE
Tel: 020-7396 5800
Fax: 020-7396 5858
Web site: *www.acca.org.uk*

Brewers and Licensed Retailers Association (BLRA)
42 Portman Square
London W1H 0BB
Tel: 020-7486 4831
Fax: 020-7935 3991
Web site: *www.blra.co.uk*

British Association for Counselling and Psychotherapy
1 Regent Place
Rugby CV21 2PJ
Tel: (01788) 550899
Fax: (01788) 562189
Email: bac@bac.co.uk
Web site: *www.counselling.co.uk*

British Chambers of Commerce
Manning House
22 Carlisle Place
London SW1P 1JA
Tel: 020-7565 2000
Fax: 020-7565 2049
Web site: *www.britishchambers.org.uk*

British Exporters Association (BExA)
Broadway House
Tothill Street
London SW1H 9NQ
Tel: 020-7222 5419
Fax: 020-7799 2468
Email: bexamail@aol.com
Web site: *www.bexa.co.uk*

British Franchise Association (BFA)
Thames View
Newtown Road
Henley-on-Thames RG9 1HG
Tel: (01491) 578049
Fax: (01491) 573517
Email: mailroom@british-fran-chise.org.uk
Web site: *www.british-franchise.org.uk*

British Standards Institute (BSI)
BSI Group
389 Chiswick High Road
London W4 4AL
Tel: 020-8996 9000
Fax: 020-8996 7400
Email: Info@bsi-global.com
Web site: *www.bsi-global.com*

British Telecom
e-business advice line (0800) 389 8878

British Venture Capital Association (BVCA)
Essex House
12-13 Essex Street
London WC2R 3AA
Tel: 020-7240 3846
Fax: 020-7240 3649
Email: bvca@bvca.co.uk
Web site: *www.bvca.co.uk*

Building Societies Ombudsman (BSO)
See Financial Ombudsman Service

Business Connect (Wales)
Tel: (0845) 7969798

Business Information Source
20 Bridge Street
Inverness IV1 1QR
Tel: (01463) 715400
Email: bis@hient.co.uk
Web site: *www.bis.uk.com*

Business Link
Signpost number: (0845) 7567765
Web site: *www.businessadviceonline.org*

Chartered Institute of Arbitrators
12 Bloomsbury Square
London WC1A 2LP
Tel: 020-7421 7444
Fax: 020-7404 4023
Email: info@arbitrators.org
Web site: *www.arbitrators.org*

Companies House (England and Wales)
Crown Way
Cardiff CF14 3UZ
Tel: (02920) 380801
Fax: (02920) 380900
Web site: *www.companieshouse.gov.uk*

Companies House (Scotland)
37 Castle Terrace
Edinburgh EH1 2EB
Tel: 0131-535 5800
Fax: 0131-535 5820
Web site: *www.companieshouse.gov.uk*

Companies Registry (Northern Ireland)
IDB House
64 Chichester Street
Belfast BT1 4JX
Tel: (028) 9023 4488
Fax: (028) 9054 4888
Web site: *www.detini.gov.uk*

Countryside Agency
John Dower House
Crescent Place
Cheltenham GL50 3RA
Tel: (01242) 521381
Fax: (01242) 584270
Email: info@countryside.gov.uk
Web site: *www.countryside.gov.uk*

Department for Education and Employment (DfEE)
Sanctuary Buildings
Great Smith Street
London SW1P 3BT
Tel: (0870) 000 2288
Fax: (01928) 794248
Email: info@dfee.gov.uk
Web site: *www.dfee.gov.uk*

Department of the Environment, Transport and the Regions (DETR)
Eland House
Bressenden Place
London SW1E 5DU
Tel: 020-7944 3000
Web site: *www.detr.gov.uk*

Department of Trade and Industry (DTI)
DTI Enquiry Unit
1 Victoria Street
London SW1H 0ET
Tel: 020-7215 5000
Textphone: 020-7215 6740
Email: dti.enquiries@dti.gsi.gov.uk
Web site: *www.dti.gov.uk*
DTI Enterprise Zone web site:
www.enterprisezone.org.uk

DSS Publications
Tel: (01253) 332222
Web site: *www.dss.gov.uk*

DTI Publications Orderline
Admail 528
London SW1W 8YT
Tel: (0870) 1502500
Fax: (0870) 1502333
Web site: *www.dti.gov.uk/pip*

EDnet (the Economic Development Network)
Web site: *www.ednet-ni.com*

Export Clubs
Web site: *www.exportclubs.org.uk*

Federation of Small Businesses
Whittle Way
Blackpool Business Park
Blackpool FY4 2FE
Tel: (01253) 336000
Fax: (01253) 348046
Email: ho@fsb.org.uk
Web site: *www.fsb.org.uk*

Financial Ombudsman Service (FOS)
For the Banking Ombudsman Scheme and Building Societies Ombudsman
PO Box 4
South Quay Plaza
183 Marsh Wall
London E14 9SR
Tel: (0845) 766 0902
Fax: 020-7405 5052
Email: banking.ombudsman@financial-ombudsman.org.uk
Web site: *www.financial-ombudsman.org.uk*

Financial Services Authority (FSA)
25 The North Colonnade
Canary Wharf
London E14 5HS
Tel: 020-7676 1000
Fax: 020-7676 1099
Email: consumerhelp@fsa.gov.uk
Web site: *www.fsa.gov.uk*

Forestry Commission
231 Corstorphine Road
Edinburgh EH12 7AT
Tel: 0131-334 0303
Fax: 0131-334 4473
Email:
enquiries@forestry.gsi.gov.uk
Web site: *www.forestry.gov.uk*

Health and Safety Executive (HSE)
Information line: (0541) 545500
Email: hseinformationservices
@natbrit.com
Web site: *www.hse.gov.uk*

**Highlands & Islands Enterprise
(HIE)**
Bridge House
20 Bridge Street
Inverness IV1 1QR
Tel: (01463) 234171
Fax: (01463) 244469
Email: hie.general@hient.co.uk
Web site: *www.hie.co.uk*

**Independent Banking Advisory
Service (IBAS)**
Parkhill Road
Somersham
Huntingdon
Cambs PE17 3HW
Tel: (01487) 843444
Fax: (01487) 740607
Email: help@ibas.co.uk
Web site: *www.ibas.co.uk*

**Industrial Development Board
(Northern Ireland)**
IDB House
64 Chichester Street
Belfast BT1 4JX
Tel: 028-9023 3233
Fax: 028-9054 5000
Email: idbni@detini.gov.uk
Web site: *www.idbni.co.uk*

**Industrial Research and Technology
Unit (IRTU) (Northern Ireland)**
17 Antrim Road
Lisburn
Co. Antrim BT28 3AZ
Tel: 028-9262 3000
Fax: 028-9267 6054
Email: info@irtu.detini.gov.uk
Web site: *www.irdu-ni.gov.uk*

Industrial Society
Quadrant Court
49 Calthorpe Road
Edgbaston
Birmingham B15 1TH
Tel: (08704) 001000
Fax: (08704) 001099
Email:
customercentre@indsoc.co.uk
Web site: *www.indsoc.co.uk*

Inland Revenue (IR)
Telephone helplines:
Electronic business: (0845) 6055999
Employers' helpline (0845) 7143143
Self assessment: (0845) 900444
Web site: *www.inlandrevenue.gov.uk*
*Look on the web site for details of your
local enquiry centre and tax office*

Inside UK Enterprise (IUKE)
Festival Hall
Petersfield
Hampshire GU31 4JW
Tel: (01730) 235015
Fax: (01730) 268865
Email: iuke@statusmeetings.co.uk
Web site: *www.iuke.co.uk*

Institute of Directors (IoD)
116 Pall Mall
London SW1Y 5ED
Tel: 020-7839 1233
Fax: 020-7930 1949
Email: businessinfo@iod.org.uk
Web site: *www.iod.org.uk*

Institute of Export
Export House
Minerva Business Park
Lynch Wood
Peterborough PE2 6FT
Tel: (01733) 404400
Fax: (01733) 404444
Email: institute@export.org.uk
Web site: *www.export.org.uk*

Institute of Management (IM)
Management House
Cottingham Road
Corby
Northants NN17 1TT
Tel: (01536) 204222
Fax: (01536) 201651
Web site: *www.inst-mgt.org.uk*

Institute of Patentees and Inventors
Suite 505A
Triumph House
189 Regent Street
London W1B 4JY
Tel: 020-7434 1818
Fax: 020-7434 1727
Email: enquiries@invent.org.uk
Web site: *www.invent.org.uk*

Learning and Skills Council (LSC)
101 Lockhurst Lane
Foleshill
Coventry CV6 5RS
Tel: 024-7658 2761
Fax: 024-7658 2738
Email: info@lsc.gov.uk
Web site: *www.lsc.gov.uk*

Local Enterprise Development Unit (LEDU)
LEDU House
Upper Galwally
Belfast BT8 6TB
Tel: 028-9049 1031
Freephone: (0800) 0925529
Fax: 028-9069 1432
Email: ledu@ledu-ni.gov.uk
Web site: *www.ledu-ni.gov.uk*

Market Research Society
15 Northburgh Street
London EC1V 0JR
Tel: 020-7490 4911
Fax: 020-7490 0608
Email: info@mrs.org.uk
Web site: *www.mrs.org.uk*

Ministry of Agriculture, Fisheries and Food (MAFF)
3–8 Whitehall Place
London SW1A 2HH
Helpline: (0645) 335577
Tel: 020-7238 3000
Fax: 020-7238 6591
Email: helpline@maff.gsi.gov.uk
Web site: *www.maff.gov.uk*

National Business Angels Network (NBAN)
40–42 Cannon Street
London EC4N 6JJ
Tel: 020-7329 2929
Information line: 020-7329 4141
Fax: 020-7329 2626
Email: info@bestmatch.co.uk
Web site: *www.bestmatch.co.uk*

National Endowment for Science,
Technology and the Arts (NESTA)
Fishmonger's Chambers
110 Upper Thames Street
London EC4R 3TW
Tel: 020-7645 9500
Fax: 020-7645 9501
Email: nesta@nesta.org.uk
Web site: *www.nesta.org.uk*

National Federation of Enterprise
Agencies
Trinity Gardens
9–11 Bromham Road
Bedford MK40 2UQ
Tel/Fax: (01234) 354055
Email: alan.bretherton@nfea.com
Web site: *www.nfea.com*

Occupational Pensions Regulatory
Authority (OPRA)
Invicta House
Trafalgar Place
Brighton
BN1 4DW
Tel: (01273) 627600
Fax: (01273) 627688
Email: helpdesk@opra.gov.uk
Web site: *www.opra.gov.uk*

Patent Office
Concept House
Cardiff Road
Newport NP10 8QQ
Tel: (01633) 814000
Central Enquiry Unit:
(0845) 9500505
Email: enquiries@patent.gov.uk
Web site: *www.patent.gov.uk*

Phoenix Fund
Small Business Service
Small Firm Finance Section
Level 2
St Mary's House
c/o Moorfoot
Sheffield S1 4PQ
Tel: 0114-259 7422/7113
Fax: 0114-259 7316
Email: mike.purdom@
sbs.gsi.gov.uk
Web site: *www.businesslink.org*

The Prince's Trust
18 Park Square East
London NW1 4LH
Tel: 020-7543 1234
Fax: 020-7543 1200
Web site: *www.princes-trust.co.uk*

Royal British Legion
48 Pall Mall
London SW1Y 5JY
Tel: (08457) 725725
Fax: 020-7973 7239
Email: info@britishlegion.org.uk
Web site: *www.britishlegion.org.uk*

Royal College of Psychiatrists
17 Belgrave Square
London SW1X 8PG
Tel: 020-7235 2351
Fax: 020-7245 1231
Email: rcpsych@rcpsych.ac.uk
Web site: *www.rcpsych.ac.uk*

Scottish Enterprise
120 Bothwell Street
Glasgow G2 1PC
Helpline: (08456) 078787
Fax: 0141-228 2511
Web site: *www.scottish-enterprise.com*

Scottish Executive
Enterprise and Lifelong Learning
Department
Business Growth Unit
The Scottish Executive
4th Floor
Meridian Court
Cadogan Street
Glasgow G2 6AT
Tel: 0141-248 2855
Email: ceu@scotland.gov.uk
Web site: *www.scotland.gov.uk*

Shell LiveWIRE
Hawthorn House
Forth Banks
Newcastle upon Tyne NE1 3SG
Tel: 0191-261 5584
Enquiry line: (0845) 7573252
Fax: 0191-261 1910
Email: livewire@projectne.co.uk
Web site: *www.shell-livewire.org*

Small Business Gateway
Tel: (0845) 6078787 (if outside
Scotland), (0845) 6096611 (if within
Scotland)
Web site: *www.sbgateway.com*

Small Business Service (SBS)
1 Victoria Street
London SW1H 0ET
and
St Mary's House
c/o Moorfoot
Sheffield S1 4PQ
Tel: 0114-259 7788
Fax: 0114-259 7330
Email: gatewayenquiries
@sbs.gsi.gov.uk
Web site:
www.businesslink.org

Stationery Office
Tel: (0870) 6005522

**Teaching Company Directorate
(TCD)**
Hillside House
79 London Street
Faringdon
Oxfordshire SN7 8AA
Tel: (01367) 245200
Fax: (01367) 242831
Email: office@tcd.co.uk
Web site: *www.tcd.co.uk*

UK Business Incubation (UKBI)
Aston Science Park
Love Lane
Birmingham B7 4BJ
Tel: 0121-250 3538
Fax: 0121-250 3542
Email: info@ukbi.co.uk
Web site: *www.ukbi.co.uk*

**UK Science Park Association
(UKSPA)**
Aston Science Park
Love Lane
Birmingham B7 4BJ
Tel: 0121-359 0981
Fax: 0121-333 5852
Email: info@ukspa.org.uk
Web site: *www.ukspa.org.uk*

Virginbiz.net
Tel: (0845) 2700 500
Web site: *www.virginbiz.net*

Welsh Development Agency
Principality House
The Friary
Cardiff CF10 3FE
Tel: (0845) 7775577
Fax: 029-2082 8912
Email: enquiries@wda.co.uk
Web site: *www.wda.co.uk*

Which? Books
Freepost
PO Box 44
Hertford X, SG14 1YB
Tel: (0800) 252100
Fax: (0800) 533053
Web site: *www.which.net*

Which? Online
Castlemead
Gascoyne Way
Hertford X, SG14 1YB
Tel: (0800) 252100
Web site: *www.which.net*

Which? Publications
Tel: (0800) 252100

Which? Software
Tel: (0800) 920140

Which? TaxService
Castlemead
Gascoyne Way
Hertford X, SG14 1LH
Tel: (0870) 0100529
Web site: *www.taxcalc.com*

The Woodland Trust
Autumn Park
Grantham
Lincolnshire NG31 6LL
Tel: (01476) 581135
Fax: (01476) 590808
Email: enquiries@woodland-trust.org.uk
Web site: *www.woodland-trust.org.uk*

Index